Dueling Banjos

The Deliverance
of Drew

Ronny Cox

Edited by Barbara Bowers

Dueling Banjos: The Deliverance of Drew

Copyright © 2012 by Ronny Cox

ISBN 10: 1-936085-59-3
ISBN 13: 978-1-936085-59-0

Library of Congress Control Number: 2011943376

Book cover and design by Sebastian Weber

Picture Credits: All clips from the movie DELIVERANCE courtesy of Warner Bros. Inc. and used with permission

Photos on the front and back cover by Dick Lowry

Felsen Press®
An Imprint of Decent Hill
Cleveland, Ohio

www.FelsenPress.com
(866) 688-5325

FELSEN
PRESS
An Imprint of Decent Hill

Also Available from Decent Hill

FOLLOW
by David Knighton

THE LOVE I NEVER HAD
by Sheila T. Williams

NO BOUNDARIES
by Brenda J. Gilham

HEALER
by Dua Yacoubi

POLITICAL LOGIC
by Larry Allen Brown

RACING WITH THE STARS
by A. J. Graziano

TRUCKER PARADISE
by Melissa Grube

DESPERATE JOURNEY
by James K. Renshaw

THE TRIAL
by Rickey McDonald

ROAD TRIPPN'
by Sean McLaughlin

RHYTHMIC ECHOES
by J. Truman Stewart

EDITOR'S NOTES

Ask anyone if they know who Ronny Cox is, and many of them will have to think about it, not sure if he is an actor, or a musician, or if they've ever heard of him at all. They usually cast their eyes skyward as they frown and think on it. But ask them if they remember the movie *Deliverance* and you are guaranteed to get a big YES. Then ask them if they remember *Dueling Banjos*, and the light bulb goes off. Of course! THAT'S who he is! Drew from *Deliverance*! No movie in the history of American cinema has struck fear in the hearts of men as *Deliverance*.

It's been forty years since the filming of *Deliverance*, and it still remains one of the top movies that can be called to mind simply with that one word. The movie was raw, emotional, violent and shocking – but it leaves a lasting impression of artistic excellence. Ronny Cox is one of the world's great storytellers, and this book follows his journey from a struggling unknown stage actor to a leap through the door of Hollywood stardom, appearing in his first film ever with the likes of Jon Voight, Burt Reynolds, Ned Beatty and director John Boorman. In his own words, he shares the wonder, the hardships, the laughter, the brotherhood... and the magic that brought to life the great novel written by James Dickey.

This book was born joyfully in a rather creative and sometimes painful way. While on a road trip, Ronny recorded these stories, sometimes while driving and therefore sometimes distracted. He sent me the recordings electronically on mp3's, which I downloaded to my ipod and then transcribed. There were stops and starts and fragmented sentences, hems and haws, incomplete thoughts, the voice of a GPS in the background, laughter, comments about red lights, left turns and the highway, and more laughter. And oh yes – there were stories. These wonderful stories, told in a way that only a world-class storyteller can tell. Every reader of this book needs to hear Ronny tell a story orally. Because my monumental task was to sort out these transcriptions and make these stories flow off the page the same way they flow from his mouth. There were many good-natured "dueling" conversations between Ronny and me as we bartered back and forth about wording and worked together to shape these stories. I do think the final product is as close as you can get to hearing each story read out loud to you by Ronny. He paints pictures of his memories and the only thing missing is the sound of his own laughter as he shares a funny tale.

It was my profound honor to have worked with him on this labor of love.

Barbara Bowers, Editor
October 2011

CONTENTS

Dueling Banjos

The Deliverance
of Drew

Ronny Cox

Edited by Barbara Bowers

THE TWO GUYS BELOW THE TITLE

In the spring of 1971, my life was about to change in the most unimaginable way in the world.

My wife Mary and I were living in Rye, New York, with our two small boys, Brian and John, and Mary was just starting the third year of her post-doctoral fellowship with Sloan-Kettering. Mary had a PhD in Chemistry from Georgetown University, and of course, I was a struggling actor and had worked at Arena Stage and had done some off-Broadway and Broadway and Shakespeare in the Park, but was basically a struggling actor. So here we were in Rye, New York, and there was this movie that was being done and I got a call to go in and meet with John Boorman about this film called *Deliverance*.

I've talked to Lynn Stalmaster, who cast the picture, and I believe that I'm the first person that they saw in New York, not because I was at the top of anyone's list, but because I was so far at the BOTTOM of the list. I think they were going to start seeing people at 10 o'clock on a Monday morning, and they asked me to come in at 9 o'clock for a pre-meeting with Lynn Stalmaster to see if I was even worth meeting with. You see, John Boorman's concept was to do the film with all unknown actors, so they came to New York looking for unknown actors, and god knows... I was unknown!

So anyway, I met with Lynn Stalmaster. I had read the novel and he gave me a copy of the screenplay. I guess he liked me, he told me to go away to a coffee shop or something and come back in an hour. So I went to the coffee shop, and since I was already familiar with the novel, I read it through really quickly and came back at 10 o'clock. I met with John Boorman, who was the director, a wonderful little Irishman, he also produced the film. We hit it off famously, so during the course of that week, they called me back in a couple more times to meet with John. We read some scenes and talked about the role and talked about the whole concept of how he wanted to do the film.

Now in those days, preliminary meetings with casting agents and directors were scheduled in either ten or fifteen minute intervals. You literally went in and said hello, gave them a picture and a resume, spoke briefly and then you were out of there. One of the ways you used to keep score when you were a new young actor going in to meet on a movie or a television show or even a commercial was how long you could push that ten or fifteen minute limit. It sort of became a badge of honor, so even if you didn't get the job, you could go out and say, "Well, I spent the full fifteen minutes in there". That became an ego boost for those of us who were struggling actors.

What was really sort of incredible that day was that John Boorman and I connected immediately, beyond the pleasantries. I spent almost a full hour in there with him, and had never felt so welcomed or felt like someone was appreciating my talent quite so much as he was. He was fascinated that I had a musical background and that I had grown up in the Southwest, as opposed to the South. I don't know what difference that made to him because this is a very Southern film that we were talking about, but John seemed to be mightily impressed with me, and I got to spend that hour in there with him.

Later that day, I got this big excited phone call from my agent going on and on about how they loved me, and that I was going to get to come back. It was a huge boost to my ego. Most of the time my agent could hardly be bothered to answer my phone calls... but now, all of a sudden without doing anything except having a meeting, I was being treated very differently.

They liked me, so within the next couple of weeks they flew a whole bunch of us from New York out to Warner Brothers in Burbank, California. They did screen tests for eighteen of us. There were four groups of four, with two people left over. We spent the whole day doing the big debate scene, sort of deciding what to do with the rapist after they had shot the guy with the arrow. As it turns out, since there were four groups and they had these two guys left over, John Boorman asked me to step in with them, and I was actually tested twice for the role. Out of those eighteen people, I was actually the only one they liked. Well... that's not really true. Bill McKinney, who played the rapist (the guy that got shot with the arrow by Burt Reynolds), was actually testing for Burt Reynolds' role of Lewis. So John Boorman DID actually like him, he just didn't see him in Burt's role. I was the only actor they liked for any of the four principle roles.

So I came back to New York and waited around for a couple weeks. I love this aspect of Hollywood. About two or three weeks later they flew twelve guys from Los Angeles to New York and tested them there – the excesses of Hollywood, I suppose. Anyway, during that screen test is where they found Ned Beatty, although he didn't actually come from California, he had come from Arena Stage in Washington, D.C.

Ned and I had done about thirty plays together at Arena Stage. I had left but he was still there. They were testing people on a Saturday as I recall, and Ned had two shows to do that day, a matinee and an evening show. When Lynn Stalmaster called him up to see if he could get on a shuttle and come and test in the morning, and then get back in time to do the matinee and the evening show, he was afraid he couldn't do it. But he did finally arrange to get a flight, got there very early in the morning and saw John. It was kind of serendipitous, because another actor friend of mine, a man named Barton Heyman, had met with John Boorman during that previous week for the role of Bobby, which became Ned's role. John Boorman had actually told Barton Heyman that the role was his, that he wasn't going to see anybody else because Barton had just so convinced him that he was the right guy for the role. But what had happened was that Lynn Stalmaster had remembered Ned, sort of at the last minute, and had cajoled him into coming up to New York from D.C. to test. So in a way, by him going to all that trouble, John Boorman in all good conscience couldn't not see Ned out of courtesy to Ned and Lynn Stalmaster.

Long story short – Ned blew him away. It was sad for Barton that he didn't get that role, but wonderful for us and the film that Ned did. Ned and I were such great good friends and had done all these plays together, and they didn't even know that we knew each other, so we were cast totally independently of each other. I was actually at that session as well because John Boorman had called me up and said, "Ronny, I don't want you to feel like you are having to test again, but I would like to have you there to bounce other characters off of." He wanted to match people up. So anyway I was there at that test and did a couple of the scenes with the guys there.

So now basically they had found Ned and me. And they still were not settled on anyone to play the other two roles. I think it may be the first time in the history of film that they found the two guys below the title before they found the two guys above the title – it generally doesn't work that way. So Ned and I waited around for another five or six weeks while they were figuring out who was going to play the other two roles. And I have to tell you this right now – every major actor in Hollywood wanted to do this film.

I don't want to drop a lot of names here, but literally, this was 1971, and you name the absolute A-list – the AAA list of Hollywood actors or New York actors, for that matter – and they all wanted to do this movie. One of the reasons that John wanted to do this film with all unknowns was that he didn't want any character to be safe. If you saw Robert Redford or Paul Newman in a movie in the 70's, and it was a movie in which the characters were in danger, you were pretty sure – pretty DAMN sure that that big star was not going to be in danger of not making it through. Well... now that I think about it, maybe these two are a bad example if you think about *Butch Cassidy and the Sundance Kid*...

So John Boorman's whole concept was that he wanted all of these guys to be at risk. Since this was such a harrowing movie, he didn't want anyone to be safe, so he really wanted to do and was prepared to do the film with all unknowns. Obviously the studio would never let them do that, I mean, you've gotta have some name to hang the film on.

Dueling Banjos: The Deliverance of Drew

John Boorman's casting in this film, I think, was incredible. His idea precluded him from using older established "big-name" actors. If you remember, in the book, all the characters were in their early forties, and John felt he wanted the characters to be younger. Now I know there is a tendency by the studios these days on a youth movement just to cast everything younger, you know, apparently because they think it's sexier or something like that. But that was not his intention at all.

His whole feeling about these guys being in their early thirties was because he had a very particular idea of why that should be. If you recall, we shot this film in 1971, and in 1971 we were just coming out of the Vietnam War, and there was a big dichotomy in this country. John Boorman felt that the most interesting guys around were the guys in their early thirties, because guys in their forties were already old enough to be part of the establishment, and younger guys in their twenties were part of the youth hippie movement. So he thought guys in their early thirties were the guys caught in the middle... they weren't old enough to be establishment, they weren't young enough to be the hippies and they were sort of the most confused and angst-ridden men in America at that time. So he very consciously wanted our characters to be in that age group.

Agents were submitting to him names of guys who were in their fifties, because in Hollywood in those days if you were fifty-five, you played forty and so they were submitting guys in their fifties to play these characters. Not only that, this was a film that required some physical stamina, which precluded some of those guys... because this was not going to be made in the traditional way where the stunt guys did everything and then the actors came in for their close-ups or whatever. John really wanted us to be doing ALL this stuff. So he was not interested in casting this in the normal way that films were cast. There were to be no stunt men in this film. We spent six to eight weeks on the river learning how to survive class-four rapids, boulders, cliffs and snakes before the first camera even rolled.

Jon Voight had just done *Midnight Cowboy* the year before. He was already established as a star. Burt Reynolds had been around for a while, but he had not really established himself as that real force that he became. The year of *Deliverance* changed Burt's career dramatically. He did three things that year that changed it: he went on the Tonight Show for the first time and people realized he was funny; he did *Deliverance* and people realized that he really was this incredibly gifted actor; and he did the centerfold for *Playgirl*. Those three things all combined made him this big star.

So anyway, you now have the two guys above the title, as well as the two guys below the title, and we're going to go down to Georgia to make this film...

Burt and Ned horsing around as Jon and I are talking.
Billy Joe Redden is walking away.

GODDAMN, THAT'S A GOOD LINE!

I've talked to John Boorman several times since the making of the film and one of the things he has said – and I take it as a great compliment to me and Ned - was that although it was great to do the film with Burt and Jon, the biggest thrill was to have these two unknowns that he really believed in to do the film. So here I am... and you've got to realize, I had never made more than $6000 in one year as an actor before that. Mary and I had lived this whole graduate student/struggling actor existence with two small boys, basically living hand to mouth - and now, they fly me down to Georgia, FIRST CLASS, and I fly into Atlanta.

Just as I got into Atlanta, they picked me up there, and whoever it was who picked me up (I can't remember now) said that James Dickey was doing a poetry reading that afternoon of his poems and wanted to know if I would like to go. And I said, "Of COURSE I would!" I happen to think that James Dickey is one of the great American poets, writing incredible muscular poetry that really captures that sort of Southern essence. I was knocked out, not only by the book *Deliverance*, but I was really knocked out by his poetry as well.

So they took me and we snuck into the back of the hall there where Jim was reading his poetry for the ladies that afternoon. Jim was a big mountain of a man, well over 200 pounds, big and hulking, and spoke with a really redolent Southern accent. And so, there he was up in front of the room holding forth. He was reading his poetry and he was so into this one poem. It was mesmerizing to hear him read the poem, and I'll never forget - he got to this one place and he read this line of poetry and he stopped and he looked up and he said, "GODDAMN, that's a good line!", and I was blown away. I said, "WOW, this was a guy who was so into his own poetry that even at that point he recognizes his own powerful line".

Not to make too big a feast of it, but I saw him a week or two later doing the same poem and he said the SAME line. Maybe it was part of the poem anyway, but it was very effective no matter what.

Now we drive out to Clayton, Georgia, which is where the film was to be shot. Clayton is a small little town on the Chattooga River where we're going to shoot this film, which is the border of Georgia and South Carolina, and North Carolina is there as well right in that corner. In Clayton, we were staying at this wonderful golf club, the Kingwood Country Club. John Boorman had a house right on the golf course.

When we first got there, they had a sort of motel that was for guests that came in, but after we'd been there awhile... at first Ned and I were just staying in a motel room on the course, and then, lo and behold, the perks of being a "movie star" kicked in, and eventually all four of us – Burt Reynolds, Jon Voight, Ned Beatty and myself all had our own houses. I had a house off the 7th hole of the golf course, and I was rattling around since I don't cook or anything. It was superfluous for me to be in a big house, but it SURE did feel kind of nice...

BEING SIMPLE IS THE HARDEST THING TO DO

Now we are there and we are ready for rehearsals. Maybe this is a good time to talk about the way we rehearsed that film. I don't mean to imply that John Boorman wasn't in absolute strict control of the film at all times, but we largely improvised that film, and by that I mean we spent two weeks of going through and breaking down every scene. As the characters, we would start with the basis of a scene, of any particular scene in the screenplay, and let them find out where they were in relation to the other characters. Each one of us developed our character through this improvisational process. At any given time in a scene, even on a take, we were free to say whatever we felt our character would say or was compelled to say. If John Boorman didn't like it, he would simply say, "That didn't work and let's do something else", with no recriminations.

All of us were drawn to try to find different ways to express these guys and we found that if you took one character out of the mix for a while it changed the relationships of the other characters. We really got to know those guys in a very VERY particular way and I think it paid off in myriad ways in the film. If Drew was not in a scene, the characters were bolder and the sensitivity my character brought to the story was lessened. If Bobby wasn't present, there was less joking around. If Lewis was gone, there was less competition. John wanted to be sure that each character's point of view always came through. But... because we rehearsed that way, it caused some sort of friction that I now have to own up to.

You've got to realize that this was not only my first film, but essentially my first time in front of a camera, and while I'd been an actor for ten years and had done plays and all kinds of other things, I had very little knowledge of films and how they were made. And since I'm not really a well-trained actor (you know I went to a small school in New Mexico), I learned acting more by just doing it than any other way. So what I have is a sense of honesty about the work. I found that honesty stood me in good stead once I learned how to let go of all the layers we put in front of honesty. Being simple is the hardest thing to do as an actor.

When we were rehearsing, I didn't know a way to approach that role, other than to become him. Drew was the sensitive one and able to relate on a person-to-person level better than any of the others, as evidenced by his connection with the kid playing *Dueling Banjos*. I sort of went into that mode and lived in that mode.

Now... believe me, I am NOT a method actor. And I sort of don't believe you have to be a drug addict or a drunk to know how to portray one. You have to be personally responsible for your character and you have to use your imagination. Because . . . there's another part of you, this actor... that has to be in the back of your mind somewhere checking and seeing how your character is doing, saying, "Oh, this works, this doesn't work". Someone has to be making those choices... someone that knows some things about the character that the character might NOT know. So... I was further toward becoming Drew than I ever would be in any character I've played since. I just sort of walked around being Drew all the time.

We were rehearsing one day and we'd actually gotten to that pivotal scene in the film after Bobby is raped, where they've shot the mountain man and they are debating about what to do with the body. I was basically saying to the guys that I thought Drew was right, that essentially the proper thing to do would be to take the body back down to Aintry, turn themselves in, tell the authorities what happened - it was CERTAINLY justifiable homicide - basically making that argument. I was doing it as an exercise after John Boorman had said, "Okay, convince us".

We literally spent an hour with me, as Drew, trying to convince these other three guys what they should do. I mean, for instance, one my arguments was that these guys weren't black... they were worried about not being able to get a fair trial from these mountain people, or worried about a cousin or a brother being on the jury, and they would get railroaded.

Well... these are good old Southern boys and they know about change of venue. They know those things and they were sort of upper middle-class guys too, so if they were concerned they knew they could wait until they got to Atlanta to turn themselves in. What it really came down to was that Bobby didn't want it getting out about the rape, obviously, and there was a revenge factor. They just wanted to bury the guy and be done with it.

In the course of this exercise for this big huge scene - in the course of an hour – and that's another thing that happens, sometimes people don't realize that when you are rehearsing you do things over the top. I spent an hour shouting, begging, pleading, screaming at these guys ... doing everything I could to convince them that what they were doing was equally wrong. If they were going to flout the law and bury this guy, it would be two wrongs that don't make a right.

I went on and on and on and ON, and it so happened that Jim Dickey was at that rehearsal. Holy shit, he thought that was the greatest acting he had ever seen. I don't think he quite realized that what I was doing was SO over the top we would never ever do that on film. It was a way of finding out what the limits were, of what things worked and what things didn't. There were many layers involved here, but I don't think Jim got a lot of that. From that moment on, he thought I was "the actor of the world", and he never ever called me Ronny. He only ever referred to me as Drew. It really got to be almost too much.

Jim was a legendary drinker, and we would be out all day rehearsing or having canoe practice and we would come in at the end of the day and Jim would be there in the bar with his cronies. I would walk in and Jim would say, "Drew, Drew, get over here – I've been telling these guys about that scene, do that scene!" He actually expected me to do a scene for a bunch of drunks in a bar. I mean... he was the writer of the film and I was in this whole Drew-sensitivity mode – I would turn him down but I worried that he would be mad at me. Well ... John Boorman got wind of this. It's a pretty well-known fact that Jim Dickey was asked to leave the set. I read in his son's book, *Summer of Deliverance,* several different versions of how and why he got kicked off. I happen to know the real reason. It was because of me.

I certainly didn't ask for it, but John Boorman had heard what was going on and he called all of us together, the four actors and Jim Dickey right before we were going to start shooting and made a very eloquent speech. He told Jim he had written a brilliant novel, that his help had been invaluable, and that we valued everything he had done for us, but now it was to the point where we needed to do the film, and it would be better if he was not there.

Jim Dickey went through the roof, practically doing all the things that I did in that rehearsal. Essentially he played all four characters for us. He spent awhile being Mr. Macho Man, playing Burt Reynold's character, Lewis; then he played the thoughtful character of Ed, Jon Voight's part, saying how we couldn't make it without him; then he played the clown, Ned's character; and then the sensitive poet came out when he played Drew. He went through the whole thing and really held forth for about an hour. He lectured and ranted – he just wasn't used to not getting his way. He really was like a petulant child. It finally came down to him saying he would not go until each one of the actors told him that they agreed with John Boorman.

You see, he thought John Boorman was just trying to pull a power trip on him. I'll hand it to the other guys – they were fabulous. They were all able to tell him that it was great to have him there but that they really needed to do this alone, without hurting his feelings or backing down. Then it came to me – and I was awful – because I knew that essentially he was being kicked off because of me. I didn't have the tools to be able to say it right. I kind of teared up and just sat there and was not really able to speak. The tears were because I felt responsible for him being asked to leave... he just thought I was a weakling. He then accepted that he was off the set.

Jim eventually left and the four of us all talked for ten or fifteen minutes after that meeting. Then we left John Boorman's, and as I walked toward my house, Jim was waiting for me. He said to me, "Drew (here again, he wouldn't call me Ronny) – I'm really disappointed in you. I know that all those other guys were just going along with John Boorman. I KNOW you wanted me to stay. All you had to do was say that you wanted me to stay, and you didn't have the guts to say it. I'm really disappointed that you didn't have the guts to say you needed me here".

So there's that lie. He was gone from the set primarily because of me, and here again he just didn't recognize or realize that I needed him gone more than anybody else did...

A great candid shot of Edward Ramey and two of the extras from the Dueling Banjos scene.

DON'T EVEN GO
NEAR THE CANOES

Alongside the rehearsal process, I was introduced to a plethora of things that I had no concept of before. All of a sudden I'm plunged into wardrobe fittings, hair and makeup meetings, and tests to see what things looked like on film. Then we started canoe practice, because there is an awful lot of canoeing that takes place in this movie. Contrary to what most people think, there is not a stunt man in this movie anywhere. The four of us did all the canoeing in this movie, and one of the reasons for shooting the film in sequence was because the easy rapids are in the beginning and they get harder as they go along.

So we had two weeks of canoe practice and then started at the beginning of the film paddling down the river, and by the time we got to the really hard rapids we had spent six to eight hours a day on the water for eight or nine weeks. By that time, all of us were pretty damn good canoeists. The four of us were all pretty good athletes to begin with. You just put that much time in and it's got to pay off.

Once we were actually in Georgia, John Boorman would take each one of us individually to work with. He took me out to one of the water hazards on the golf course, the most placid water you've ever seen in your life. The crew put a canoe in there and John and I got in the canoe – I had never been in a canoe before – and we started paddling around. It was also a private time for John and I to talk about his vision of the film, and how it was going to affect the two of us. I'm sure he had the same conversation with the other guys as well, but basically he told me he was happy to have me on the film, that he thought I was right for the role and that I would be good in it. We both acknowledged that I was a novice and knew nothing about film acting.

He was being reassuring to me, saying, "Ronny, I chose you because

I really think you are the right person for this role", telling me not to worry about the things that I didn't know. He promised me he would worry about those things and make sure that my character's point of view always comes through, and that he would protect me. He said that his heart and his intellect were really with the character of Drew, and would make sure that my character was always well-served in the film. He said, "All you have to do is worry about being Drew. Just be Drew. I will worry about everything else". It was a really reassuring time for me, and he did this with all the other guys, I'm sure.

They brought in this wonderful guy named Charlie Wiggin who was our canoe instructor, and he would take us down to the river and we started the really daunting task of learning how to look like we knew what we were doing in the canoes. I'll never forget that first day. We had the canoes and started to get them out, and he said, "NO, no, NO, don't even go near the canoes!" He took us down to the edge of the river, where there were rather frightening rapids. The water was moving rather quickly and he said, "I want you to jump in the water and go through those rapids just swimming, just you alone".

We all looked at him really strangely and he explained, "Look, unless I miss my guess, we're going to turn over a LOT in this film, and one way or another you're gonna go through the rapids. It's better if you go through in the canoe, but you're gonna go through in or out of the canoe. There is really not going to be anyone to help you, and if anyone is really in a position to help you if you go out of the canoe, they will be in the shot and it won't work. So you are always going to be out there no matter what kind of shot we are doing, and you have to figure out a way if you turn over the canoe to negotiate the rapids until you get to a place where you can get out".

He said the LAST thing you try to do in the rapids is actually try to swim. You want to get your feet in front of you, keep your head up, and just try to protect yourself. Protect your head at all times. Preferably on your back, and look for the V's in the water – that's where the most water is going through, and it's the deepest and less likely to have rocks or snags. You just keep working your way through there. In any set of rapids there's always a little backwater place after you get through where the current is not nearly as swift, and once you get to one of those little places like that, you go over to the side.

The main thing you do, if you go out of the canoe, the FIRST thought you have is try and kick that canoe and get it as far downstream from you as possible. Most people try to stay with the canoe, and that's where they get in trouble. It's not a tragedy for the canoe to be downstream and pinned up against rocks and for you to be pinned up against it. The tragedy is if YOU are downstream and now the canoe comes sideways and it will crush you. You can be pinned against a rock, the canoe can hit you in the head – there are a million ways to get in trouble by trying to stay with the canoe.

You don't want the canoe to be upstream from you. If it's going one way, you go the other way if you can, and forget about the canoe. Charlie said, "We can find other canoes, that's the least of our worries". So having said that, he made us all jump in the water and go down through there.

Now I'm a strong swimmer and so were the other guys, but this is a different kettle of fish. This has nothing to do with swimming and it takes you awhile to be able to deal with the power of that water. That was the other thing he impressed upon us. You'll find out as soon as you get in how much power there is in that water. You must respect that power. Once we went through the rapids just in our skins, then Charlie put us in the canoes and taught us the different strokes to keep it going straight down the river. There are J strokes and draw strokes and you are basically trying to keep the canoe going straight down the river. When you get in trouble in canoes is when it gets sideways. You try not to ever get sideways to the current, and you must always read the river. At any given time, that was the most important thing.

When we finally started shooting the film, Charlie would canoe down through there to set the camera angles for the crew, and our assignment as actors was to walk along the edge of the river and watch the line that he would take getting through the rapids. Often times he would make a mistake – he would choose the wrong line - and he would come back and say, "Do you see where I made a mistake? Don't do THAT – come this way".

After a while when we were shooting, we would come back and we were more concerned about if we got a good grade from Charlie about our canoeing, rather than if the shot was okay. In a lot of ways, it was almost easy to forget that we were actually making a movie...

A HAPPY ACCIDENT

We were outdoors for basically every scene in this film and the cameras had to be set up in such weird places. That's another thing we found out - when we were doing the tests for filming, we discovered you could be in the most horrendous rapids and sometimes on film it looked almost placid. And especially when an expert like Charlie canoed through it, it looked almost languid, and didn't have the drama at all that John Boorman wished for the film. So we did a lot of tests. We had to find what angles worked the best and added the most excitement to the film. We discovered that the closer the lens was to the water, the better the shot was. In other words, down on sticks just barely above the surface, almost at water level, it really made it much more exciting and dramatic.

I might as well own up to this, like I said, I'm from New Mexico and even though I'm a strong swimmer, I was not real comfortable with the concept of this white water. The first couple of times we went out they shot tests of the four of us in canoes paddling along, and believe me, these were not really heavy rapids. There was a little white water, but not much. Burt, Jon and Ned were making the strokes and doing great and looked fabulous. Even as slow as the water was, I was making way more paddle strokes and making it more dramatic than the others.

We were reviewing the test shots and John Boorman said, "Guys! Watch Ronny! It's way more exciting the way he's doing it than the way guys you are doing it!" The guys ragged me a lot about that, saying, "Okay, we'll try to be panic-stricken like Ronny is!" I kept telling them I was just "acting" – the whole idea was to make it dramatic and they didn't let me get away with that.

Also during this time, even though we were wearing one set of clothes because the movie all takes place in two days, it was the first time I really realized how much thought and effort went into wardrobing each person so that there was a reflection of that person's character. It was the first time I was really cognizant of how much goes into that aspect. Most people probably don't know, but right before I was doing *Deliverance*, I had been doing a play in which I portrayed a Germanic character, and for the play my hair had been bleached almost white-blonde. As you know, Jon Voight is blonde as well, and we have practically the same body-type build. We're both about six feet two, and weighed about 175 or 180 lbs. Since we were in the canoe together, they were a little concerned that on first look people would not necessarily be able to tell us apart.

I only found out about this after the fact, but I probably owe my role in *Deliverance* to Ned. When they called to tell him he had the role of Bobby, he asked, "What about Ronny?" Apparently they told him then that they were uncertain because of the physical resemblance to Jon Voight at that time with my light hair. Ned said, "You don't think he is blond, do you?", and then went on to assure them that I was actually reddish-blond, my sideburns are red, and my mother was a redhead. Within the next hour they called me up and offered me the job. So for the film they dyed my hair almost black and I wore glasses and a hat. Jon grew a mustache just so there were other ways at a glance to identify us.

While I was going through all these machinations, there was another thing being worked out. Since Drew dies in the film, they were working the way that his body would be discovered in the water. I was being fitted with false eyeballs because they wanted to find Drew face-up in the water with his eyes open. As they were fitting me, I happened to say to John Boorman "You know, I can do a really strange thing with my shoulders". And he said, "What?"

When I was very young, I had a minor case of polio, and as a result of that, both of my shoulders would come completely out of place. I'm older now and I can't do it so much anymore. The way they find me in *Deliverance*, with my arm over my head – everybody thinks that's some sort of prosthetic or some sort of terrible makeup thing. That was just my arm and I was doing that. So when I showed that to John Boorman he almost fell down – he just thought it was the greatest thing in the world. So instead of having to be fitted with false eyeballs, I could just do this instead.

I'll just tell you a little bit about this. As an illustration of what I could do with my shoulders - I could take my right hand and put it over behind my head and wrap it all the way around and scratch my right ear. Or I could take my right hand over my shoulders and actually get a book of matches out of the front pockets of my jeans. I used to win bets in college from guys. I could clasp my hands in front of me and step through my hands and bring them behind me and all the way back to the front without ever ungrasping my hands.

So many people who have seen *Deliverance* think that the scene with my arm was just the most amazing makeup feat in the history of the world. We had a wonderful young makeup artist named Michael Hancock. He used to call himself Hancock of Hollywood. I'm not sure if this was his first film but it certainly was one of his early films. To tell you the truth, they didn't envision a lot of makeup of any sort or special stuff on this film. None of the four of us were really wearing makeup because we were in the water all the time, and John Boorman wanted to do this movie very realistically and naturalistically. The only reason we had Hancock was to do the broken leg of Burt's, and to fit me with my false eyeballs, which went away. And just basic film makeup, that's it.

When the film came out, Mike Hancock got all kinds of accolades for this spectacular special effects makeup that he did. People would ask him, "How did you do that, Mike, HOW did you do that?" and he would just smile and say, "It's a trade secret, I can't tell you." For several years after that he got known as the guy who could do these really macabre things and it really was kind of a boost to his career. His career was going to take off no matter what – he is now Morgan Freeman's make-up artist and he's a brilliant artist. He and I have laughed about it a couple times since then. Basically all he did for my shoulder was just put some blue makeup on there to make it look bruised and stuff like that. The actual arm being out of place... that I could just do. I did all the rest.

I have read reviews by several film critics that thought John Boorman was really playing with deep-seated symbolism when he showed them finding Drew's guitar and the neck of the guitar was broken, and then they found Drew with his arm broken in the same way. They drew great parallels of symbolism there. I never thought too much about it, although several people have told me it turned their stomach. I thought it was interesting... it was just kind of a happy accident.

Vilmos filming the mangled body. Yep... that's really my arm.
Pretty good trick, huh?

YOU CAN CALL ME
SQUINTY EYES

Now it's time to talk about the other actors in the movie. The film has gotten a lot of accolades for being shot down in Clayton, Georgia, and nearly all the actors with the exception of the four of us were found right down there in Clayton. You will recall that Bill McKinney tested for the role of Lewis and wound up playing the rapist, and of course Jim Dickey wound up playing the sheriff. There was a professional actor who wound up playing the deputy. The Griner brother who drove the car down to Aintry was actually a wonderful New York actor named Seamon Glass. I thought he was really really good in the film but unfortunately he had a New York accent, and they had to eventually revoice his character. They brought in another actor to voice over, and he did a really good job. Normally when you revoice an actor, it jumps out at you like a sore thumb, but this was really well done.

Edward Ramey, the old man who did the dance at the service station, the doctor who patched up Burt Reynolds at the end, the young boy, Billy Joe Redden – we found all of them right there in Clayton. When we get back from the trip and Drew is dead, and Jon Voight and Ned Beatty are back at that boarding house having dinner with all those people – there's a wonderful family restaurant in Georgia called Dillard's. They catered the film for us, we took their good old home-cooked meals with us every day on the river. So when they did that scene of the dinner at the boarding house, that's a lot of the patrons from the restaurant in that scene, and the lady serving was actually Mrs. Dillard. Normally when you get people trying to play themselves there is a self-consciousness about them. The brilliance of Lynn Stalmaster's casting and of John Boorman's incredible direction was to put them at ease so they could do what he asked them to do without being self-conscious. I didn't know any better then, but in my forty years of film since then, I've never seen amateur actors be able to do that quite as well as they did.

Now we'll talk about the casting of Billy Joe Redden. The character that plays *Dueling Banjos* in the movie is named Lonnie. They had interviewed a lot of young boys to play that character, and since he and I were going to do the scene together, they always had me be there for us to play off each other. We met with several little kids – some of them were quite good. At the very end of the movie when Jon Voight's character comes back to pick up the cars there is a little boy who comes out and says, "Are you here about the cars?" and Jon Voight says, "Yes" – well, he was one of the kids that they auditioned. As a matter of fact, they thought they were going to use him and he was a favorite. And then one day Billy Joe Redden came in, and I'm not absolutely positive about this, but I believe he was only in the second or third grade at the time, and he was 13 or 14 years old! He came in and met with us and we talked with him as much as we could, he was completely closed off, it was really hard to get to him. But we all loved him and the look and the smile worked so well, that sly look of absolute innocence showed through. Once we met with him we all looked at each other and John Boorman said, "Well, I think we've found our Lonnie".

John Boorman's only concern was whether or not he would be able to take direction. That was his concern with ALL of the locals. You can meet with them on one level but whether or not you could ask them to do something and have them follow through was a different thing. They set up a couple more meetings for Billy Joe to come back and see if it would work. I have to tell you - I fell in love with Billy Joe's take on the character from the get-go. When they said they were seeing other kids, I said, "I don't want to hear about it!" - I wanted him and no one else.

At some point, John Boorman came to me and said, "Ronny, I don't think that we're going to be able to use Billy Joe" and I said, "Why why WHY??", and he said, "Well, we've tried to work with him and I just can't connect with him, I can't get on the same page with him, and I'm just afraid that we'll never be able to get a performance out of him." I actually begged John – we still had about a week before we were going to start shooting. I said, "You have this other kid as a back up that you can go to at the last minute, and you know he could do it". I asked him to let me work with Billy Joe for a week and see if I could get through to him.

So they sent a car for Billy every afternoon, picked him up from school and they would bring him out to me. He and I most of the time would just go walk in the woods and talk and do stuff, and he was just as closed off to me as he was to John for the first two or three days. We were going along and it just seemed fruitless, he was stoic and within himself and I just couldn't connect. Then . . . I don't even know HOW it happened, but I remember the day it happened.

You normally think of Southerners as speaking really slowly. Well Billy Joe spoke so fast that you could hardly understand him. For some reason one day we got to talking about guitars – he was telling me that he had a guitar at home, and he says, "Yeah, yeah, yeah, I got a guitar at home, got no strings on it, I gotta get me some strings, how much do them strings cost, 'bout fifty cents? I don't like to carry that much cash!" All of a sudden a flood gate opened and he started talking to me about school and his frustrations about school because I guess he had been left a couple of grades behind and stuff and people teased him at school and he would say, "Yeah – all them damn guys they all call me squinty eyes, I'm gonna kill the next sonbitch that calls me squinty eyes". And then he did the most endearing thing. He put his arm around my shoulder and said, "Cept YOU, Ronny. You can call me squinty eyes if you want to cause I like you GOOD." And sort of from then on we were like best buddies. There was a vivaciousness about him and an openness. I excitedly went to John Boorman and asked him to come and observe how we were interacting and he could see it was working, so he decided to use Billy.

One of the things I am reticent to talk about but happy to at the same time is this... because Billy related to me so well, we discovered when we started shooting the scene that Billy would only look at the person talking to him, and primarily would only look at me. You have to realize, here I am – I know absolutely ZERO about making movies, about anything. The way that opening scene of *Dueling Banjos* worked with me and Billy was that John Boorman had to come and would whisper in my ear what he wanted me to tell Billy and I had to stand there and tell Billy what John Boorman had said. I'm sure the crew was sitting around thinking WHAT is this guy doing, because it looked like I was actually directing the scene. It was out of pure ignorance. John would tell me what to tell Billy to do, and I would tell Billy and then he would react and do what he was supposed to do.

One other thing that I feel really proud about was after we finished playing *Dueling Banjos*, when I asked Billy if he wanted to play another one – he was supposed to look mean at me and look away, and they kept trying and he COULDN'T look mean at me. Well, he actually didn't like Ned Beatty very well, so we had him look at Ned instead and look mean, then look away. I felt good about him not being able to look mean at me.

Once the scene was finished – and it took a week to shoot it - it was very complex with a lot of different angles and cuts, and they realized they had gold there and milked it for all they could. John Boorman took me aside and said, "Ronny, I think Billy Joe's performance is magic, I think it's all incredible – and I want to give you credit, I think we owe a lot of his performance to you, because you were there for him." I think it had more to do with Billy Joe doing a marvelous performance, but I'm flattered and honored that John thought I played a major part in it. I am proud of the scene, we worked well together, and if I had anything to do with Billy Joe's performance, then I'm proud of that too...

PADDLE FASTER,
I HEAR BANJOS

Because we shot in sequence, the *Dueling Banjos* scene was the very first scene shot in the picture. The filming of this scene was fascinating and magic, and people have wondered for years about it being filmed. Many are convinced that it was a spontaneous event, that we came upon this kid and I was fooling around on my guitar and he started playing back what I played. The cameraman saw an opportunity to film this "unrehearsed" scene and had enough sense to turn on the camera, and then of course, it was put into the movie. Well, there's not a bit of truth in that story.

I was cast in the movie because I play the guitar, but I am not a hot bluegrass picker, I'm not even what you consider a picker. I play a three-finger percussive picking style. While I am a fairly good guitarist, I am certainly not a good enough guitarist to play that piece, but John Boorman sort of didn't care about that. Billy Joe couldn't play the banjo, couldn't play it at all, so we were always going to have to pre-record the song. Billy Joe and I would have to match the playback, in other words, we would film and we would act as if we were playing it. When it came time to record the song, John Boorman came to me, he REALLY wanted me to play it, and he said, "Ronny, I need you to go in to Atlanta tomorrow and record the song" - but it was my first film, my first time in front of a camera, and I'd have to miss a day of rehearsal and miss a day of canoe practice. We had Eric Weissberg and Steve Mandel down there, because not only did they play *Dueling Banjos* for the scene, all the other music in the film is variations on that theme and they were there to play all of those as well. None of us thought about this being a hit song, as a matter of fact, Eric Weissberg when he came down said, "Why are we doing THIS piece of shit, why don't we do something good?"

So I actually begged John not to make me play it. Even if I recorded it in Atlanta, I knew I would still have to fake play it when we shot because I would have to match the playback – but John Boorman said, "You don't understand, Ronny, I want to be able to cut to fingers actually playing the right notes. So I want you to be playing it, because since Billy Joe can't play at all, I'm never going to cut to his left hand, which is the fingering hand, I'm only going to cut to his right hand so he can be faking that he's doing all the picking with his right hand. So when I cut to hands playing in the scene, I'm going to cut to your hands, so I want you to be playing the right note, and it's going to be better for the film". So I said, "John, I can do that, I'll match the playback exactly and if I make a mistake I'll tell you . . . I'll say don't use that take, I'm not playing the right note there". He really wanted me to be able to finger the exact notes, he thought it was really important for the scene.

John Boorman wasn't really interested in making a number one hit song as *Dueling Banjos* became. He didn't care if I wasn't a great joe-pro guitar player, as a matter of fact, he kind of liked the idea that I was an amateur guitar player and that I was being completely shown up by this young savant that was playing the banjo. So it didn't bother him at all that I couldn't play nearly as well as Steve Mandel could play. Although, had I done it in the film, we probably wouldn't have had a number one hit song.

The filming of the *Dueling Banjos* scene was fascinating, especially for a novice like me, but people through the years have actually been fascinated by the process of making that magic scene come alive. It was rife with any number of technical problems. I spent the better part of two days just going over and over the recording that Eric Weissberg and Steve Mandel made, making sure that I was playing the right notes at the right time. Since Billy Joe didn't play, they actually didn't even put real banjo strings on his banjo, just rubbery strings that wouldn't bother his fingers. The point was that John was most of the time going to cut to his right hand and my left hand, which was playing the notes.

The way it worked was that I was standing on the ground, and Billy Joe was up on a porch about four feet in the air, sitting on a porch swing.

Since he didn't know enough about the banjo to make it look like he was playing, the way it was shot was that he would tuck his left arm in behind him as tightly as he could. Another little kid who knew something about the banjo was on his knees behind the swing with a wardrobe shirt on that looked just like Billy's and he stuck his left arm around him. It was so awkward that they had a prop guy hold the kid up so he could reach his arm around and pretend to do the fingering on the banjo. I've seen a wonderful photograph, a side view of me standing on the ground with my guitar, Billy Joe on the porch, the little kid behind him, and then the prop guy holding him up.

There are close to sixty or seventy set-ups for all of the various angles of that scene because the scene does go on for quite awhile. With all the coverage, you have to see the scene from Jon Voight's point of view, from Ned Beatty's point of view, from Burt Reynold's point of view, from Edward Ramey, the old man who did the wonderful dance there, and the mountain men who were down there whistling and carrying on. You think that it's a four, five, six minute scene once we are actually playing. The filming of that one scene took the better part of a week. It was an eye-opening experience for me, who really didn't know anything about film at that point.

After the movie came out, I once played *Dueling Banjos* with Roy Clark on the Dinah Shore show, and I messed up, as an amateur guitarist would. I'm not a real picker and it was kind of funny at the beginning, but when it finally takes off and the banjo really sings, then it didn't matter anymore and the audience went crazy for that song. So who knows . . . if I had actually played the song in the movie, we might have had a number one hit anyway. When push comes to shove, that's not me on the soundtrack, that's Steve Mandel on the guitar. I probably cost myself a whole bunch of money, because that song went to number one on every chart in the world for a long time. It really is a remarkable piece of music to play.

The Saturday night before we were shooting that scene, Eric and Steve came down and went to the local dance in Clayton, Georgia. Eric and Steve are these two New York guys, but great pickers – they took their instruments and during the break, went up to the bandleader and said they were here shooting the movie that's in town, and they asked if they could sit in and maybe play a tune or two - and the leader of the band said, "No, if we let YOU, we'd have to let EVERYBODY play". So here are two of the greatest musicians in the world being turned down by these local guys in Clayton, Georgia.

One other interesting fact – the original title of *Dueling Banjos* was called *Feuding Banjos*. It was played by a couple of guys at a folk festival in Oregon several years before we started the movie. The song was actually written by a man named Arthur "Guitar Boogie" Smith several years earlier. Warner Brothers may have thought it was public domain, but they did not credit him or pay royalties. Now this is a song that is going through the roof, not just in country charts, but pop charts, European charts, every chart you can think of. So Arthur "Guitar Boogie" Smith called up Warner Brothers and said, "That's MY song, you owe me royalties", and Warner Brothers decided to fight it in court. It strung out for several years, but I'm happy to say it was settled in favor of Arthur. So now he gets all the royalties from that.

The song is one that is familiar to everyone, no matter who you ask. To this day, you see t-shirts that say *paddle faster, I hear banjos! Dueling Banjos* has sort of become in the vernacular for all kinds of things that happen in the South. Some Southerners resent us for that, but others know it was a great boon to the South...

It takes a village to play the banjo.

THERE'S NO ACTING
IN CANOES

White water canoeing is really hard. Especially when the canoe you have is not really intended for white water. According to the story line of the script we had one aluminum canoe, which is intended for white water, and one Old Town wooden canoe, which isn't. It's a lake canoe and not really suitable for white water at all. It has a very deep draft and is narrow, with not much stability or not much freeboard. Anytime you are in any sort of pretty good white water, you are in danger of taking on a lot of water because it rides so low in the water. Whereas the aluminum canoe has a very shallow draft and is very wide and stable and can shoot through, almost go over the rocks because it's so flat on the bottom. All the places that the wooden Old Town canoe would get caught up or run over rocks and stuff, the aluminum canoe could go right over.

Ned and Burt were in the aluminum canoe, and Jon Voight and I were in the wooden Old Town canoe. It's no exaggeration to say that Jon and I turned over and wrecked about sixty percent of the time. First of all, we were just beginning to learn to do the stuff and we were also in a canoe not intended for white water. So it got to the point that when Ned and Burt would run a set of rapids, if they had any trouble at all, the crew would lay big bets that Jon Voight and I would wreck. Which we did. We wrecked a LOT.

When we first got there and started shooting, we each took along two or three sets of clothes in case we got wet or anything like that, and we also had battery packs with microphones - lavolier mics. They are expensive mics that we were wearing so they could record the dialogue. Well, after we dumped two or three times the first day and were trying to change clothes all the time and had essentially ruined about six or eight of these expensive microphones and backpacks for the microphones, they decided we would wear the same clothes all the time. If we started to shoot a scene and we were dry, we would just wet ourselves down so we would always match and every scene from then on was with our clothes wet. So we didn't have to worry if they were dry clothes or wet clothes – they were always wet. And then they just did away with the microphones and also came to a decision that we would eventually just loop everything.

That's another thing we all came to realize – that there is no acting in canoes. When you are going through white water, there's no acting, you are trying to stay alive and have your wits about you, so we never played a scene while we were paddling through rapids. We would always get through the rapids and then pull into the side and then they could boom us or whatever and get the sound that way. Any incidental things that we happened to say while we were going through the rapids we would eventually go back and loop those. In other words, we added the dialogue later.

It HELPS to know your left from your right. And what we discovered - not only were Jon and I turning over a lot of times, we were making a lot of mistakes. I was getting blamed for this because well, I was the guy below the title, and not the guy above the title. We would dump or we would turn over and something would go wrong and we would come back and John Boorman would say "What happened?" and Jon Voight would always say, "Well, Ronny did this and did this and did this... " and I didn't know for sure if I DID that, I was just trying to stay in the canoe. I was basically getting the blame for us turning over all the time. Because essentially the guy in the front – me – was supposed to read the river and point the nose of the canoe where most of the water was going.

You always look for the V's, that's where all the water is going. So my job was to do a draw stroke to the right (where you sort of reach out and pull the canoe to the right) and there's another thing called a J stroke that pushes it to the left. Those are essentially the two strokes for moving the bow of the canoe. And the guy in the back of the canoe, in the stern, his whole thing is to actually act as a rudder. Wherever the nose goes, he was supposed to make sure the back of the canoe stays in that line so that you're always going straight. So here again, we were turning over a LOT and I accepted that I was doing it – UNTIL...

... after we've shot for a day we send the film back to Los Angeles to be processed and we get it back a day later – that's what they call the dailies. And so then we would go and watch the dailies and see if the scenes were okay or not. Well, don't you know, we were watching the scene where we were dumping and doing all the stuff. This happened to be the scene in the movie where Jon Voight and I are going through a set of rapids, and we turn around and go through the rapids backwards. We crashed rather badly there and actually broke the canoe in half. It was a pretty harrowing experience. Later we went back and put in a scene where we laughed about it in calmer water, like ha ha ha, we went through it backwards. But when we actually did it, it wasn't funny. While we were watching that scene, we see that much to our surprise, Jon Voight made exactly the wrong maneuver. He was the one flipping us around backwards! He is a wonderful athlete and a really good canoeist, except in times of stress he doesn't know his left from his right.

Sometimes we just couldn't do it because a wooden Old Town canoe just wasn't intended for white water. But the places where we were messing up most of the time were because Jon was making the wrong stroke. That came home to roost later in the film. Drew had already drowned and they had buried him, and Burt Reynold's character Lewis is in the bottom of the canoe, and Jon Voight and Ned are paddling on down the river. By this time we are into some really pretty heavy rapids. There's a place there called Woodall Shoals – it's a class four rapid. For a canoe, that's really hairy stuff. When they were doing that, Burt was supposed to be in the bottom of the canoe, and they didn't even have him in there, the angle was high enough that you couldn't really see what was in there. So it was just Jon Voight and Ned Beatty going through Woodall Shoals, which is a really hairy section of the river.

Ned, as per the script, only really has a little half-oar that he's paddling with and was in the front. Jon was in the back, and they're negotiating this horrible set of rapids – and we actually have this on film... they were going along, and Ned was working, working, working and Jon keeps making these wrong moves, and pretty soon Ned looked around at him with the MOST exasperated look on his face... looks at Jon, looks at his oar and throws it into the water, and says, "Okay, you're NOT going to listen . . ." and then he sits there with his arms folded, waiting for the crash. And they crashed, of course!

We all wrecked a lot – Jon and I crashed more than the other guys did. Since there were no stunt men, it was dangerous. We had a big meeting about this before we started shooting, none of us wanted to not be safe – and even with the best of intentions I almost drowned once and Ned almost drowned once on the film. So we had this agreement going in that any set of rapids that any of us didn't want to do, we just had to say, "I'm not doing it" and no questions asked, we wouldn't do it. Everybody said absolutely right, that was the agreement we had. The only problem was that no one guy ever got spooked at the same place any of the others did. Sometimes the worst-looking rapids were the easiest to negotiate and sometimes the most innocuous-looking could really be killer rapids. So you never knew really where the danger was.

There was the place where Jon Voight and I had turned around and crashed very badly, breaking the canoe in half. We had done that scene right at the end of the day as the last shot. We finished up and went in and spent the night. I hardly slept at all that night... I had nightmares all night about that scene that we were running. I dreamt that I drowned there the next day, I kept seeing this hydraulic where I got caught, like a whirlpool but vertical, pulling me up and down. I just couldn't sleep, and had such a vision of me drowning in this pool of water.

So the next day we canoe to that same place and we're going to shoot that scene again, because obviously we crashed the day before. I was just freaked, I didn't want to do it, and I said to the guys, "Guys, I'm not going to do this". And all of them, to a man, said, "Oh you shouldn't Ronny, you shouldn't, you ABSOLUTELY shouldn't do it, if you're spooked by this and freaked out by this, then you absolutely shouldn't do it. But you know something Ronny? This seems like a piece of cake to ME, so I'M going to do it. So you don't do it – don't even WORRY about you doing it, we're going to get another guy and just put your clothes on him, and we won't ever film him, we'll shoot the other three of us... "

Well then, of course, pretty soon I was cursing them and saying the whole way, "Okay, goddammit, I'll DO it"... and now we're going through there and it's just like my dream is being re-lived. Jon Voight and I turn over in exactly that place and that hydraulic pulls me down for just half a second and then spits me out. It really was nothing! It was like my dream came true but only to the point where I went under the water, and then all of a sudden reality sets in. I came out, it was great, and I felt so relieved. So Jon and I got back in the canoe and ran the same thing again, but didn't crash this time and we had a great shot.

And that's how the other guys would be. Sometimes we'd get to places and they would say, "I don't think I want to do these rapids"... but the other three of us would say, "Ah, THIS is no big deal, just watch us". And as it ended up, all four of us did all the canoeing all the time. By the end of it, we all became really good canoeists.

I would say probably that Ned Beatty was the best canoeist of us all. Jon was a great athlete, he would just get confused with right and left occasionally. I was pretty good. But Burt... I have to explain this in a very particular way. Burt couldn't be bothered with learning the proper way to do stuff, because he just wanted to do everything his macho way. So often times they would go through awful-looking sets of rapids, and he would just set his mind to it and go forth. Burt in that respect was the best of us all. Just through pure athleticism and pure, "By god, I'm going to DO this and this river can't stop ME", he did it. I'll always have a really special place in my heart just for that kind of ego that says, "I can DO this"...

Burt and Ned going through a really harrowing set of rapids.
Miraculously, they didn't crash. Jon and I would not be so lucky.

HE'S A MOVIE STAR
AND HE'S JUST LIKE US!

Whenever a major film like *Deliverance* comes into a small town a lot of things happen, most of them good. It's a great economic boon to the town, the restaurants do more business, the motels and the hotels are full, all the businesses, the laundries, the bars, and the film company spends a lot of money there. Even in 1971 it infused a quick million dollars into the little town of Clayton, Georgia.

Also a lot of the local people worked as extras, or in construction, or as drivers. It's a great boon to the town on the one hand, and a source of great tension on the other. Here a Hollywood film crew is coming in and we are outsiders, and there is a great deal of suspicion of anyone coming from the outside. Most of the locals had not read the book and had only heard about the more salacious aspects of the book. A great many people there thought we were almost making a porno movie and there was a sort of reticence to even have anything to do with us on that level.

There were also eighty to one hundred guys on the film crew, they're away from home, so they have a tendency to go out and drink and relax at night, most are away from their wives and families, and that creates tension too, because they are flirting with all the local women and local men get upset, and invariably there are always some sort of liaisons that happen between locals and the film crew which causes great tension. Often times there is a danger of fights in the bars and a resentment of the film crew invading their town. So on one hand it's really good economically, but on the other hand you have all these outsiders that are disrupting their way of life.

One of the things that I discovered was since it was my first film, and I'm a musician, is that the universal way to reach people was borne out by playing my guitar with the locals. In a way it's almost borne out in the film too, when Drew plays guitar with Lonnie. When I had any time off I would go into town and often take my guitar, and go to a bar where a lot of the locals and I would sit and share music. There is a profound one-on-one sharing that can take place through music. Music cuts straight to the heart – it cuts through everything else. It gets through barriers like nothing else can. I found that I was able to relate to the locals in a way that the others couldn't.

I don't mean to sound self-aggrandizing at all, it's just that I was able to communicate in a way that the film people and other actors couldn't. I was such a novice at this, and through no fault of their own, Jon Voight and Burt Reynolds were "movie stars" and there was a certain sort of awe that people regarded them with and they were somewhat unapproachable because of that. With me and Ned, although Ned was not as forthcoming as I was about going out and mingling, people would say things like "Ronny's a movie star and he's just like us, and that's okay!" So it seemed I was accepted more and didn't feel as much of the tension.

I talked to a lot of the crew and the other actors and they always felt when they went into town and went into a bar or a restaurant there was an undercurrent of tension that was there because of the underlying suspicion. I found that I didn't feel that. There was an openness and a friendliness. Also, being from the Southwest gave me an advantage because it's the same sort of culture where you speak to everyone on the street, and when you say how are you, you REALLY want to know rather than just a cursory nod. Coupled with the music being shared, I just really felt at home there and didn't feel alienated as some of the other guys did...

I GUESS
I DONE WORSE

I thought the casting of the film was remarkable. I want to talk a little bit about the men who played the menacing characters in the show, the mountain men. Seamon Glass came in from New York and played the main Griner brother. Then there were two other Griner brothers – when we drive down to the river and there are three brothers in the truck. One of them was a young man named Randall Deal, he and I became really good friends. We used to play music together. One day he brought in some white lightning and shared it with me. Now I am not really much of a drinker at all, and this white lightning did some pretty amazing things to my brain. In the course of our talking with each other I found out there was a lot of moonshining going on in Clayton, Georgia, and Randall may have even served a little time for moonshining. It just seemed to be a way of life to him.

The other guy in the truck was a gentleman named Howard Blalock. He had been cast and he was to work two days. Apparently, he had had some kind of minor run-in with the law, either a DUI or a parole violation or something – so those two days we were supposed to shoot with him he was actually spending that time in jail. So the producers arranged it with the sheriff to let him out during the day to come and film and then he would go back to jail at night. That created a bit of a problem because someone at the jail had apparently read or heard about the novel and was telling Howard about the more lewd aspects of the film, and told him that he was actually going to have to "DO" that, that there was no acting involved, he was actually going to have to participate in these depraved sexual scenes. So Howard wouldn't come to work that morning. We were an hour and a half late getting started because they had to send an emissary to the jail to convince him that this was acting and that there was nothing that he was going to have to do that was untoward. So FINALLY he came out.

That was another real problem for John Boorman and Lynn Stalmaster when they were casting this. They were trying to cast these hillbillys, especially the other guy in the rape scene, and they had a lot of local men come in and they would meet with them to see if they were interested in playing that character. It was a fair piece of money for a rural town, but they had all heard these stories about the rape scene. They didn't need to be great actors – turns out they got a great actor, but because Bill McKinney had most of the lines, John Boorman didn't feel like they had to be great. He met with four or five guys and had actually offered them the role, and they turned him down, partly because of the nature of the material. One guy said to him, "I couldn't do that, if I did THAT, how could I look at my mother?" So they just had a really hard time casting that character.

Finally Burt Reynolds, who had grown up down in Georgia, remembered a guy that he had known when he was in college. They had worked either construction or in a mine together for a couple of summers. He got in touch with Herbert "Cowboy" Coward, and he came in and met with John Boorman. By this time, John Boorman had been snake bit enough times that he sort of started the conversation with a fairly direct question. He asked if Cowboy knew what it was about, and Cowboy said, "Yes, Burt told me". John asked him if he would be okay with playing that role. Cowboy, who had a slight stammer – although it's funny, he never stammered on camera - said, "wwwwwwwwuullll, I guess I done worse!" So then we had our guy and he ended up being the source of some of my favorite stories from the movie, he was such a wonderful character.

I don't think, according to Burt – and if I'm wrong, I'll apologize to Cowboy - he was actually that literate. I think someone had to read him the lines and he learned them by rote. He also negotiated his own contract, and I'm not sure he had ever seen a television set. This was 1971. I don't know what his salary was, but one of the perks was to be put up in a hotel with a television and they had to keep his bathtub full of Budweiser beer on ice. That was part of his pay. He would come home from filming, take off all his clothes, sit on the commode, turn on the television so he could watch and sit there naked, reach over and grab a beer and sit and drink and sit on the throne, and that is how he spent his evenings. Pretty good life!

Cowboy and Bill McKinney
in a lighter moment behind the scenes

SNAKES FREAK ME OUT
& BUCK FEVER

As we were approaching the beginning of actual filming on the river, canoe practice became much more intense. We had graduated from swimming through rapids to going through in the canoes. Then about two days before we were actually going to start shooting, Charlie put each one of us in a canoe alone. His feeling about that was if you knew how to navigate a canoe absolutely alone through the rapids, it would stand you in good stead in case something happened and you were the only one there. It was an exercise that was pretty challenging for all of us.

It's one thing for two men to go through there, but to do it alone, pointing the bow toward the V where most of the water is and then getting the rear of the canoe to follow along was a very daunting task for all of us. We spent the better part of a couple of days, all four of us, dumping in the water a lot. We weren't in a really heavy section of rapids, but heavy enough and challenging enough that we all sort of felt like we were taking our lives in our hands. The thing that you do find out when you dump in the canoe is that if you just get away from the canoe as far as possible and get through the rapids, there's always a little eddy there, a little backwater place, and you can get into there.

Now one day we were there, and I remember this well. I have been around rattlesnakes all my life. I have to say, even though I've been around them all my life, they kind of freak me out. As my dad used to say when I was a kid in New Mexico, a rattlesnake may not hurt you but they can make you hurt yourself! Which was pretty true! One day the other guys had each gone through the set of rapids alone, and all of a sudden it was my turn. I'm negotiating there and just working so hard and concentrating on trying to get through this set of rapids and I'm heading to this V, going between these two rocks, they were sort of flat rocks and they came up to about eye level. Just as I got right between them, I looked over to my left and there is a water moccasin, looking right at me, and he couldn't have been more than eight or nine inches from my face.

Now - I have no recollection of this, but the guys all tell me they were watching me go down through this set of rapids and it seemed like I was doing okay and all of a sudden they said I just leapt out of the canoe and was flailing in the water. I have NO idea how I got there. The bad thing was that I startled the snake too and he slithered off the rock and so now he's swimming in the water. He wasn't that close to me, maybe six or eight feet away, and was certainly not coming toward me, but we were both going in the same direction, and that freaked me out even MORE. It took several minutes to regain my composure after we got back to the shore.

During this time as well, while we were doing this individual canoe stuff, I was practicing on the guitar, and Jon Voight and Burt Reynolds were having bow and arrow practice. The days were filled with activities getting us ready to do this film. Actually both Burt and Jon became quite good with the bow and arrow. One of the hardest things to do with any sort of control was in this one scene in the film where they talk about buck egger (buck fever). That's the phenomenon where you pull the bow back and see your target there and become so rife with tension that you start shaking uncontrollably and no one really knows where that arrow is going to go.

Burt didn't have to do it so much because his character was not supposed to have suffered from that, but for Jon Voight it was a plot point. That second morning in the film he gets up earlier than everybody else and goes in the woods with his bow and arrow and happens upon a deer. In his attempt to shoot the deer with his bow and arrow, he suffers from buck fever, and of course misses the deer badly and it sort of shakes him. Obviously it pays off plot-wise later in the film. I watched Jon rehearsing that, and that was an incredibly difficult thing to do. We were actually using razor point arrows, and they were quite dangerous.

What I'm really pointing out is that great attention was paid to every detail in the movie. I really felt like we were prepared for this film in the BEST possible way...

John Boorman and Jon Voight lining up the "buck egger" shot.
Note the camera is angled right on the arrow.

POINT A TO POINT B
LIFE IMITATING ART

The day before we were to actually start filming, Jon Voight and Burt Reynolds came to Ned and I and explained to us how lucky we were that we were going to get to shoot this film in sequence. Both Ned and I had come from the world of theater and plays, and obviously in a play, you start at the beginning and you do the play and you go to the end. Movies are almost never made that way. The reason for that always comes down to the budget. Normally in most conventional films, the scenes take place in several different locations. So during the course of a movie when they are filming it, every time they go to that location they are going to film every scene that takes place at that location, no matter where it falls in the script. It makes sense monetarily to do it all at once and to only set it all up once.

There's another reason. Sometimes you might have a really key actor who is only in a few scenes. They might hire some really well-known star to come in and play those few scenes. Sometimes those scenes are here and there, and so you want to shoot all of those scenes at once, especially if it's an expensive actor so you don't have him on the payroll sitting around twiddling his thumbs. There are any number of reasons why you shoot out of sequence. Maybe there are only certain days you can get a location. For instance, sometimes if you are shooting in a place of business or a mall, you might have to shoot on a Saturday or Sunday when they are closed.

Deliverance was different in lots of ways. First of all, there were only four of us, we didn't have an expensive actor that we had to get in and get out, and we were there the whole time. In terms of location, this is a film that starts at point A and goes to point B, and it never goes back to the same location twice. So there is no reason to shoot things out of sequence in that respect either. We were allowed the luxury of shooting in sequence, and it pays off in so many ways that you can hardly iterate the number of ways. In a normal film, if you scratched your cheek going down the river, and the next day you were shooting a previous scene, you would have to cover it with make-up. Or if you bumped your knee in a scene that's previous, you would have to suck it up and not limp the next day. By shooting this in sequence, if you scratched your cheek, well, now you had a scratched cheek. If you bumped your knee, well, now you could limp. If you tore your shirt, well, now you had a torn shirt. They all worked for this film.

It paid off in ways we didn't even foresee. The scene after Drew has drowned and the mountain guy is on top of the mountain is an example. Jon Voight's character is climbing up the mountain and there is a wonderful close up shot of Jon's hand pulling himself up on the ledge. Included in this shot, he has on his wristwatch. By that time we had been canoeing for several weeks and the face of the watch was completely fogged over in that one shot. You would probably never think if you were doing that in a traditional movie way with what they call an "insert shot", they would never think to fog over the watch. While it doesn't scream at you that this is more authentic, subconsciously the viewer knows that this is a much more naturalistic point of view that we're dealing with here.

We'd been in Georgia for about three weeks rehearsing and practicing, doing wardrobe and shooting the *Dueling Banjos* sequence. At the beginning of the fourth week we were finally going to get on the river for real. At that time the Chattooga River was such a pristine river, and the challenge often times was finding places to get in and get out. They literally had to sometimes use four-wheel drive or even caterpillars to put us in at point A and we might film to a certain distance down the river. When we get to the end of the filming day, we STILL might have to canoe another ten miles or so to get out of the river because there were only a certain few places where we could get in and out. It was also logistically really hard because we had canoes and we had to take a sort of skeleton crew. We had two or three big rafts for the little bit of lighting equipment and lenses and cameras and crew guys. So often times, we had to take the barest of skeleton crews. A couple of days we had to leave the script supervisor back. That's the guy who's in charge of continuity and we would have to come back at the end of the day and tell him what shots we did, what lenses we used. With today's technology he could have been connected electronically, but in those days there was no way and I remember - he was dismayed that he was going to be responsible for continuity and often didn't get to go along with us.

So we would put in and go down the river and the river was so pristine. We'd try to find a place to shoot, and they would go ahead with the camera rafts and set up. They wanted the lenses to be down as close to the water as possible to give the shots more drama. So once they were set up, we would come and canoe past them.

What we discovered very quickly was that there was no way anyone could help you once you were in the water and the cameras were set. It became a ritual for Charlie Wiggin, the expert canoeist, to go and canoe down first so they could get the camera angles and he would also read the river. That's half the deal, reading that river. Often times he insisted on us walking along the bank as much as we could and watching the line he took and watching the river at all times. The river changes from minute to minute, and you always want to go where the most water is going so you're not in danger of getting into the rocks. Sometimes Charlie would choose the wrong line and would come back and say, "You see where I went to the left and into that rock, DON'T go there, go to the right, that's a better line", because once he got out on the river he could see it and we would make mental notes. And if he had any problems at all going through there, then Jon Voight and I were GUARANTEED to wreck. We turned over a LOT.

One of the things we found when we were looking for places to get in the river was an instance of life imitating art. One day we were out there just basically looking for a point to get in, and all of a sudden out of the woods come about ten or fifteen guys with rifles. It was kind of scary, because those guys obviously had not heard that we were a movie crew and I'm pretty sure they were doing moonshine. I think they thought we were federal guys, revenuers, and they came prepared for a battle.

Luckily we had a local guy with us, Tom Ricks, our local liason, who knew them all. They didn't exactly come up to us, they were sort of ringing around us menacingly. Tom went over and talked to them and we could only tell by the gesturing and things going on what must have been said. Tom told us later that he had to do some pretty tall explaining, since they saw that we certainly were outsiders. It took him the better part of a half hour to make a good enough explanation that they accepted, and when he came back toward us and he was telling us about it, we looked around and they were just gone. They just disappeared.

In many ways for us actors, that made the playing of the rape scene WAY more important to us. In a way, it allowed us to underplay that scene I think more than we would have. When you are really frightened, there is a sort of quiet panic that takes place rather than the over-emoting of acting. So while I hate to put it this way, in some ways this was a boon to the acting in the film.

We had to take food for the crew and the actors from the Dillard's restaurant with us in containers every day as we went down the river. We would just find someplace to stop for lunch, and break out that food. Now Ned Beatty was, and is, a real outdoorsman. His goal had once been to hike the Appalachian Trail with nothing but a knife and maybe some matches to build a fire. He knew ALL the edible plants. So often times, they would just send basics with us for lunch and Ned would disappear into the woods at lunchtime and pretty soon would come back with all these greens and roots and things that were all edible and delicious, and those were our salads. This was the early 70's before a lot of people were into natural foods, and at first a lot of the guys weren't too sure they wanted to eat some of this stuff, but no one ever got sick or had any problems. It gave me a whole new appreciation of Ned's expertise.

There was one incident that happened to the lenses. To this day we don't really know what happened. We had a big raft that carried the cameras and lenses. They had case after case of lenses and they cost hundreds of thousands of dollars. We were going through these sets of rapids, and the big raft often had trouble getting through. It got caught up on a sharp jagged rock, and the rock ripped the bottom out of the raft, and they lost about four or five cases of lenses into the river. The water wasn't terribly deep there, but we had no way to get to them that day. We marked where they went in, it was just past a set of rapids that we all knew very well.

Often after you go through a set of rapids like that there is a bit of a hydraulic there and it gets deeper, so it might have been 20 or 30 feet deep, but never more than that. They were sending guys back the next day with diving equipment to retrieve them. When they went back, they searched the rest of the day and never found those lenses. There were ALL kinds of speculation – none of us could believe that there was a strong enough current, especially that deep, to wash those cases away. None of them could weigh more than 20 or 30 pounds and they wouldn't float. The only thing we could figure was that someone must have seen the raft lose the lenses and somehow during the night they had come in and gotten those lenses. But they are very particular lenses for Panavision cameras, with serial numbers, and you would think that somehow if someone tried to sell them they would turn up. They finally had to write it off for insurance and we never got them back. It cost us a little bit of time in shooting because all of a sudden there were a whole bunch of lenses that we didn't have.

Now I've been thinking about those lenses a lot. A friend of mine told me that the lenses are in foam rubber for protection and that's got to float sooner or later... but I bet they floated way down the river and that's the reason they've never shown up. Mind you, this is just speculation on my part about the reason they never showed up... but MAYBE some of those guys found those lenses and they are using them as big fancy telescopes for their rifles...

THE
PUCKER FACTOR

The only place we didn't actually shoot on the river was where Drew went out of the canoe and we had the big canoe wreck and Drew drowns. That was actually at Tallulah Gorge. They have a dam there and the reason we shot there instead of just being on the Chattooga River was because they could shut off the water at the dam and they could go in and build all the tracks for the canoe wreck. The way the scene worked was one canoe runs into the other and splits in two, and that's when we all went into the water. This was really probably the most dangerous stuff that we did in the river. First of all, my character Drew has taken off his life vest, so I'm going to have to go into this water without a life vest. A lot of things are going to happen here.

For starters, they shut off the water there and built the tracks. We rehearsed without much water coming through, and then what they were going to do was open up a gate of the dam and when the water got to the level where we wanted it, then we would shoot the shots. So we rehearsed, we got our marks for where I was supposed to go out of the canoe, of how the canoes would break in half – we had all those marks. And so now we rehearsed it with minimal water going through and then they opened up the gate of the dam. None of us were prepared for THIS much water! There was SO much that they had to move the lenses back because they were going to be swamped with water.

I had rehearsed going out of the canoe, but ALL of a sudden with this much water coming through I am to the place where I am supposed to go out of the canoe. Before I even have time to think about it, to try and save the shot, I went ahead and went out of the canoe, and I hit my shoulder. It pushed us WAY to the left from where we thought we were going to be, with all this water rushing through there. You just can't imagine how much water there was and how much power that water had. So it pushed us to the left, and when I went out of the canoe I hit my shoulder on a rock that was about six inches under the surface. It didn't break it or anything – but all of a sudden, I couldn't even USE my arm, it just sort of paralyzed my shoulder. I was really unable to swim and completely out of the channel that had been mapped out for shooting this scene.

I am now going down through this river and you have to realize that big falls is right below that, I have NO life jacket on, and the water is taking me faster than I can even imagine. They have two ropes strung across the water. I was supposed to go swimming along there and reach up and grab the rope to keep myself from going over the falls. There was another safety rope (in case I missed that one) another forty or fifty yards down. All of a sudden I look up and there's the rope and I reached up and grabbed the rope, and there is SO much water pressure I can't hold onto it. It sweeps me off of that and now I am going down to the last rope, and if I miss it, it's DEATH - I'm going to go over those falls! And those falls are 150 or 200 feet down.

So now I look up and they're no longer filming me because the camera doesn't see Drew anymore after he's out of the canoe and we're all just trying to get OUT. So I've missed the first rope and now I get to the second rope and grab the second rope – and there's too much pressure there, I CAN'T hold on to that one either and it swept me right off. Now I am literally within 40 or 50 feet of going over those falls! There was an assistant prop guy named Jerry who had tied a rope around his waist in anticipation of any problems. When I got swept off that second rope, he jumped in the water and got to me and he grabbed me and the crew pulled us back to safety. Otherwise – I'm a DEAD MAN! If I had hit my head on that rock instead of my shoulder . . . well, there would have been a lot more brain damage than I have now.

It was a pretty harrowing time. Charlie Wiggin, the expert canoeist guy, always said you count the river by "pucker" factors – that's how much your anus puckered when you were frightened by whatever you were doing with the river. So if it was an eight pucker factor, that was pretty good! I almost drowned there. Everybody got in trouble there.

They could dial the water back a little on the falls, there was almost a natural slide down through there. The way Burt actually did the slide over the falls was with a strap – they had put pitons into the side of the rock there, and he went in and held onto this strap while they opened up about an eighth of a gate of the dam to let in not quite as much water as when I went out of the canoe. There was still a lot of water coming down through there, and when the water built up to an acceptable level, they gave Burt a signal, and he let go and slid down about fifty feet into this pool at the bottom. We were all really REALLY concerned with his safety, especially after the day before with me almost drowning. He did actually hit a bump with his butt and had a big old black bruise for eight or ten days.

The way the shot was working was the lens was looking at Burt and the shot was following him as he was sliding down. Ned and Jon were standing on the rocks at the bottom of the waterfall, and they were going to dive into the pool as Burt is sliding down and then you would see all three heads pop up and you would just assume they had all gone down. All of us were really concerned about Burt because the other guys were just diving into this pool at the bottom. So Burt goes down, hits his hip on the way down, Jon Voight dives in, Ned Beatty dives in... now we're watching and Burt pops up, Jon pops up and Ned DOESN'T pop up. As it turns out, with all that water coming down through there, it created what's called a hydraulic, like a whirlpool, only it goes up and down. Ned had apparently dove too far into the center of that hydraulic and he couldn't get back up. We could all see him about five or six feet under the surface of the water fighting to get up. But the current kept pulling him down. And it seemed like FOREVER.

No one is worrying about filming anymore. Guys are jumping in the water to try and get him and they can't get under the surface to get to him. Then all of a sudden Ned disappeared. We thought he had just drowned. Then to our great surprise, fifty feet down the river he popped up! What had happened was as long as he was fighting to get up in this hydraulic, it kept pulling him back down. As soon as he finally relaxed and went down to the bottom, an under current shot him downstream and he came up. Now here's the REALLY sick thing about this. Ned and I were sharing our stories about drowning and he said his very last thought as he was finally giving up and going down was, "I hope they can find a way to finish the movie without ME". That's truly an actor's ego!

This wasn't the only danger that we all faced during the filming of this. I had almost drowned and Ned had almost drowned. When Jon Voight was climbing up that mountain to shoot the hillbilly, that scene was in the gorge as well. He actually scaled that 150 or 200 feet of sheer face of the cliff. There were several places along there, ledges and such where they could get a limited camera crew in there. So they are filming Jon as he is climbing up this mountain face and as he got up there, there was a wonderful grip named John Anderson on a ledge, basically there just to hold equipment, he wasn't there for any other purpose than to do his job. Jon was climbing up this sheer face and they were up a significant distance, 30, 40, 50 feet, and Jon had a fairly good perch with his feet. He reached up to grab a rock to pull himself up and there was this terribly slick moss. He grabbed this and he could feel himself losing his grip – it was one of those things where he kept trying and trying to hold on but he could feel himself losing his grip. So he said matter-of-factly, "I'm going to fall" – and John Anderson, the grip below him on the ledge that was maybe a foot and a half wide – reached out and caught him as he fell perhaps five or six feet. If the two of them fell, they might have died. This would have been a SIGNIFICANT fall. And here was this heroic grip who really had every reason to get out of the way with a big guy coming down on top of him but he stepped under and caught him.

The only guy that really never got in dire trouble was Burt. It just seemed that Burt by dint of will was not going to allow anything to get in his way. To me, that is a trait of Burt's that is both admirable and endearing. All of us really got a taste of what it was like to have our lives in danger. And I think that's the reason why, forty years later, even though sometimes the four of us go a couple years without seeing each other – there is always a feeling of brotherly love with all these guys. Because we all went through and sort of risked our lives together. And there's something about doing that. Not that we ever thought we were going to be in trouble – we didn't. It's just that things HAPPEN when you're on a river.

THE MYTH AND
NOTHING BUT THE MYTH

I guess it's time to talk about all the myths surrounding *Deliverance*, especially in terms of the myths involved in the making of *Deliverance*. If I had a nickel for every person that came up to me and said they either coordinated the music on *Deliverance* or they were Burt Reynold's stunt man, or they did this or did that on the movie, then I'd be a rich man. There have been so many accounts. I don't really know what that phenomenon is. I guess you take a hit film like that, and people somehow feel that they had a proprietary interest in it somehow. I'm forever having people come up to me and saying, "Oh yeah, I was THIS or I was THAT on that film"... and I'm not saying that I have a perfect memory, but I have a pretty damn GOOD memory. Everything about the making of this film is sort of indelibly etched into my memory, so I question a lot of these people.

I read a whole big long account of a person who claims not only to have been a stunt man and done all these things on *Deliverance*, but who was really the technical advisor and set up the stuff, even did all the pre-planning and working out all the logistics, originally wanted us to shoot in Alabama. And he commented on the making of the film that he had to come in and rescue the film that was going badly, that John Boorman was really ticked off with the people he had and wanted to bring in somebody who REALLY knew how to work on the river and really knew how to make things work. As far as I can figure out, this person had just written so many things that are absolutely false that I don't even know how to respond to it.

Also – these were impossible things. I'm there with the other guys and for us not to even recognize this person's name as being our "stunt man" and "canoe instructor", and setting up the shots to work right is just pretty much made up out of whole cloth. I think this person might have been one of James Dickey's cronies, and I suspect that maybe early on when they were going to decide to do the movie, a lot of those guys that were friends were all sitting around shooting the bull about how the movie should be made. That may be one of the conflicts that Jim Dickey had with John Boorman, in addition to getting in the way of my performance on the film and just being a general nuisance around the actors. I have no proof of this.

I think Jim Dickey just thought he was just going to come down and that he was going to dictate how things were done pretty much as he had done in writing the novel. It was going to be made according to his whims. I think that's just part and parcel of Jim Dickey's life, he loves being this "larger than life" persona that just knows how to do everything and certainly knows how to tell everybody HOW to do everything. It should be THIS way and it should be THAT way, and I think that while he is a masterful writer and poet, I think that his knowledge of film was really minimal. So my guess is that probably this person that I've read this account from might have been in some of the early meetings with Jim Dickey when they were discussing how they were going to do the film. That's just a possibility.

Another thing. James Dickey's son, Christopher Dickey had written a book on the making of *Deliverance (Summer of Deliverance)*, which came out several years ago. He's written five or six books and is a wonderful writer in his own right. Everybody is entitled to their own stories, I have no quarrel with Christopher Dickey's stories from his point of view. Just in terms of truth to me it bears NO resemblance to any sort of truth that I know. I have a feeling that since James Dickey was kicked off the set, there was a sort of a real need to put the Dickey family "spin", if you will, on the reasons for him being kicked off the set, and also really trying to solidify James Dickey's belief that we ended up making a good film in spite of kicking him off the set.

According to the book, we ended up making a good movie just because Jim Dickey forced us to do a good thing, even though we tried to mess up the film, it ended up being okay despite our best efforts. Christopher is entitled to his stories, but they are HIS stories. In terms of honesty here, being Jim's son he was given a job on the film as a production assistant or something. At the time he was 19 years old, and while he was around, he was not in the key meetings or privy to the stuff that I'm talking about in this book. He may have heard stuff from the prop truck. I hung out with the crew a lot, that's where you sometimes find out what a film is all about, but a lot of these assertions that they made in the film and some of the stuff they've talked about just don't square with my recollections from the film.

I do want to talk a little about one stunt man. There was a guy named Ralph Garrett, a highly respected Hollywood stunt man and a good friend. He came down to Georgia and was there obstensibly to do some of the stunt work once we got to Tallulah Gorge and places like that. But I have to say that what had happened was that the four of us had done ALL of our own stunt work all the way through, and there was no way anyone could match the physicality. There are a couple of shots of Ralph Garrett that are more as a double for Jon Voight than anything else. There are a couple of long shots of him scrambling up the side of that mountain. In film, often times we have things that are shot from a far enough angle that you can just recognize the wardrobe of a person and sort of the general idea of a scene, and you shoot that from a long distance. We send out a second unit, so it's not even the main camera unit. Bill Butler, who was doing the second unit camera work went out with guys – and even this person that I was talking about before who says he was a stunt man – perhaps they did some second unit work. Although I have yet to see anyone in a second unit shot that I recognize other than the four of us.

Also these people that talk about doing all these things... they always point out that they did it TOTALLY uncredited, say they were called stand-ins, or whatever. We had a couple receptions on the film where some of the local people were invited and were around, and those people might drop some names. But to say that they were there doing the stunts, the canoeing and white water rapids that Burt, Jon, Ned and I did just doesn't make sense. And this person that I read the account from also didn't mention Charlie Wiggin at all. If you were dealing with us in canoes and didn't mention him, then you weren't THERE dealing with the canoes...

THREE BOWIE KNIVES
AND A POCKET KNIFE

I feel like in a way I have given James Dickey a little bit of a short shrift, and I just don't want anyone to ever think that I didn't admire him both as a man and as a poet. His problem with the making of *Deliverance* was the problem any of us would have had. He had written this wonderful novel and he had a vision. And being a professor and poet, I'm sure he didn't have a clue about how to make a film. Also you have to realize that James Dickey had a tremendous ego, and to give up any sort of control was almost beyond his knowing, almost just wasn't in his DNA. That was also the other thing about Jim, he was a highly competive man. He'd been a running back in college, a big football player, and he seemed to want to compete at everything in his life.

For instance, I happen to be a guitarist. Jim could play quite well. He always traveled with five or six guitars, and he would take them out and play at a moment's notice. He was good, but he wasn't as good as he thought he was. The primary problem was that if you were at a place where music was being shared, he couldn't stand for the focus to be anywhere else. While he would ask if you knew a certain song, all he meant was that he wanted to play that song and for you to get out of his way. So he would suggest all the songs, and he certainly didn't want you to play something that he suggested. While I'm not a great guitarist, I am a GOOD performer. I know how to do that stuff, and that was a source of great tension between Jim and I when we would be someplace where there was music being played. He was certainly as good a player as I am or maybe even better, but he didn't know how to be the entertainer that I am.

If I'm honest, that's one of my biggest assets. Almost without thinking, I know how to do that, how to command the audience's attention and how to entertain people. It's almost an effortless thing for me to do. I think it was not an effortless thing for Jim to do. So that caused some problems for us.

After Jim had been asked to leave the set and we finally made it through to the end of the film, it was now time for the sheriff to enter the picture. Jim Dickey played the sheriff and played it quite well, I might add. There was a real sort of simple quality to his performance, and anyone that knows me knows that that's the quality of acting that I love and admire the most – the ability to be simple. To be simple, you can't hide behind complications. You just have to do it. It's very hard, especially for non-professional actors, to grasp that. Always actors tend to make sub-conscious comments on the character they are playing instead of just very simply doing the lines and letting the character speak for himself. So I will say this for Jim Dickey, he did that very well. And by that time we were practically finished with the film and nearly all of the rancor of his being asked to leave the set had dissipated. It was really quite a cordial reunion when he came back, and everybody greeted him as he did us, with open arms.

The two or three days that he worked at the end of the picture were really great. Also when Jim came back, I think as a peace offering for having blown up the night he was kicked off the set, he came back bearing gifts. For each of the other actors, Jon, Burt and Ned, he brought a beautiful bone-handled bowie knife, wonderfully crafted, he had to have spent a fortune on them, in leather scabbards with their initials engraved. Each one of them got one of these knives, which was incredible and well-received by the guys. I don't know if it's because Drew was the sensitive one, or what... I don't know the reason why, truly – I appreciated it, however - he gave me a pocket knife. It was a beautiful little pocket knife, but it was a very different knife from what he gave the guys. I happened to have liked it better.

To this day, I don't know what I would have done with a bowie knife. I still have this pocket knife. It has a beautiful bone handle and is a truly remarkably fine knife. And I think probably as expensive as the other guys' knives were. I just found it curious that he gave me a pocket knife when he gave all the other guys a bowie knife...

TRUSSING UP
THE DUMMY

Now I'd like to talk in earnest about Cowboy Coward. He was the guy that Burt found for us and was a local guy. He turned out to be a really brilliant actor and a really funny witty guy. We never could figure out for sure – he loved to put on this air of being a country bumpkin, if you will – and you never could be certain that he wasn't pulling your leg at the same time that he was being a buffoon. He was a source of some of the funniest memories I have from the film. He was that second rapist – the one that got away.

Bill McKinney's character of course died. So now after the canoe wreck and we've all dumped in the water, and Drew is missing, Burt's leg is busted, and Burt's character Lewis keeps saying that Drew was shot... they are there at the bottom of this gorge absolutely exposed to the cliff above. The whole point was that if there is a mountain man up there on the top with a rifle, they would be sitting ducks if they try to leave. So at first they think maybe they will go out at night but they realize they couldn't possibly go through the rapids in the dark, especially with Lewis's broken leg. So they come to the realization, as we all know, that Ed is going to climb up there and get this other mountain man.

We've talked about Jon climbing up that mountain. When he got up there, of course now they are filming the scene where he shoots that mountain man with his arrow after having this buck egger. I love the way the movie unfolds that way. It's shot in such a way that you don't know if the arrow actually got to Cowboy's character, he keeps walking and cocking his gun – and it's only when he turns sort of in profile that you realize that he's been shot. And in the meantime, Jon Voight's character Ed has fallen on one of his arrows and has punctured his side about an inch deep and he has to actually pull that arrow out. So he's pretty well wounded there. Actually the point of this for the movie is that Ed has to find some way to move him and dispose of the body. He can't just leave that mountain man up there. He also realizes several things. The mountain man has teeth, and the guy down at the rape scene didn't, and although he checks and there is a plate... but did the guy go back and put a false plate in after, did he take that time? Also the guy down at the rape scene didn't have a ring on. This guy does have a ring on. It's creating doubt in our minds, and it's doubt that we'll deal with a little bit later. The doubt also is that he can't leave that mountain man up there to be found.

So he has to get him down to the bottom, and he has a rope with him. The plan is to truss up this dead body and lower him down into the gorge below and somehow sink him in the water so that the body has disappeared. That's about 200 feet down a sheer face. They weighted a dummy and were trying everything they could to make that dummy look like a real person – and it just didn't work. It's so obvious when it's a dummy, I mean how many movies have we all seen where they try to do that, and it takes you right out of the film if it is so obviously a dummy. They tried for the better part of a morning trying various ways of weighting the dummy so that it looked passable.

Now, I promise you, strictly as a joke – they were trussing up this dummy and Cowboy was standing nearby, and John Boorman said to Cowboy, "Cowboy – do you think YOU could do this?" And we all expected him to say something like "in your dreams", or whatever, but.... Cowboy looked at the dummy for about ten seconds and said... "Wull... if HE can do it, I guess I'll give it a try!" So they actually trussed up Cowboy and lowered him over that cliff. Now – he is up about 150 feet and he is completely hogtied, and if something goes wrong, he is a dead man. First of all, the fall would probably kill him, but once he gets to the bottom he would have NO way to swim being trussed like that, even if he survived the fall. So the courage that it took for Cowboy to do that was unheard of. And if you look at the film they lower that body and there is a weight to that body. The way his foot hits a rock and bends his leg up and it comes back as only a real limp body can do – that makes the verisimilitude of this film, the naturalism of this film pay off in ways that other films can not even approach. So a lot of those kinds of details we ended up getting almost by accident, just sort of happening on the moment. They added so much to the naturalism and scariness of this film.

Another perspective of the film on top of the cliff was this: you will remember when Jon Voight woke up that first morning and went out in the woods with his bow and arrow and saw a deer and got buck fever, panicking so much that he couldn't shoot. And when he finally did shoot the arrow he missed the deer by a mile. Obviously that sets up this scene when he's up on the cliff and he's about to shoot this mountain man and he starts getting this buck fever again. He's shaking uncontrollably, and as we find out later, his character actually does hit the mountain man this time. But when they were actually shooting the scene, they were shooting a close up of Jon Voight experiencing this buck fever, drawing the bow back and not being able to let go.

Believe me, Cowboy was not even involved in this shot in any way in the world. This was a close up of Jon Voight. Cowboy had to be thirty or forty feet away off to the side. He was just over there, looking off into the woods and just not really paying attention to the shot at all. And if you recall, they wanted these arrows, especially for this close up shot, that had razor-sharp points. They started the shot with the razor-sharp arrow and then racked focus back to Jon Voight's face and the angst that he's going through. He finally shoots this arrow, and Cowboy is standing way off to the left, and the arrow goes zinging through there and it hits a tree and ricochets. Cowboy is standing in profile, and he had his mouth slightly open and that arrow came through and nicked his top and bottom lip as it went through, just the tiniest trickle of blood. And here again, if that had been just another inch, it would have gone right through his face. Without skipping a beat, Cowboy looked over towards where the arrow had come from and sort of waved and said, "Good shot, buddy"...

THE CORPSE IS SHIVERING HERE

After they buried Cowboy in the water, that's all we shot at Tallulah Gorge, and we went back on the river. This is where they found Drew drowned. In some way, I know this sounds weird, but this was kind of scary and freaky in lots of ways too. Even though we were shooting this in the summer in Georgia and it was hotter than hell, that water was COLD. When they find Drew, he is sort of pinned up against the rock and tree branch with his shoulder all broken and mangled, and of course, that was really my shoulder out of place wedged into this place.

Typical of films, it takes a long time to shoot any kind of scene like that. There was a lot to do, first they have to find Drew, then they have to examine the body - Ned's character is trying to figure out if he was shot. Through the years that has been the source of any number of arguments and speculations about whether or not Drew was shot. Some people have come to me and are adamant that he was shot; others say he committed suicide by not wearing his life jacket. When we were actually doing the film, John Boorman came to me and said, "Ronny, Drew can either be shot or not. You can make that decision, but just promise me one thing. Make it ambiguous." Because he wanted that question. And I think I must have succeeded with the whole thing with all the arguments that have been going on around it.

I have my own theory about what happened with Drew. First of all, Drew is too strong a Catholic EVER to have committed suicide. If you recall, he argued from the depth of his soul for them to go down and turn themselves in, whatever consequences of the law, to face it... and he truly believed that. There's a revenge aspect that comes into it, but Drew just really wanted to do the right thing. Once he was voted down (he being a believer in democracy went along with the votes of the other three guys), and they took the mountain man back into the woods and buried him... when they got to that point, Drew almost dug harder in a frenzy, almost snapped, trying to get the body buried. The guys sort of went at a pace, and Drew was frantic. My feeling about that is that he was denying every core belief that he had in doing this and sort of had to put himself in another place. When he was coming back to get in the canoe after they had buried the mountain man, he didn't put his life jacket on. I don't think it was out of any sort of death wish, he was just sort of in a trance. He was just going down through there.

My feeling about this whole debate of whether of not he was shot... if you recall, at one point he sort of shakes his head and goes in the water. Now - was he not paying attention? Did his oar hit a rock? Obviously in shooting it I had to propel myself out of the canoe, but I tried to do it in a way that didn't look like it was on purpose. My own personal feeling about this is that he just wasn't paying attention and went out of the canoe. So when they found his body, they checked his head very carefully for gunshot wounds and there were none, and this creates the key moral dilemma for the entire picture. What if the guy up there on top that Jon Voight shot with his arrow was the WRONG guy? What if Drew wasn't shot? What if that was just an innocent guy up there? What if they've taken the time to go up and kill an innocent man? That makes the moral dilemma ten times greater. I think that was John Boorman's intention for having it be ambiguous of whether or not Drew was shot.

Back to them finding Drew's body. All this time I'm in this cold water. One of the things we found there was that you can sort of keep yourself warm if you were moving around a lot. But – I being dead – I was not allowed to move. We spent a day or two shooting that whole discovering Drew scene, discussing what to do, and doing the eulogy when they put rocks on him and sank him in the river. So I am there with my shoulder out of place, in a terribly uncomfortable position, although there really isn't any pain – just keeping your shoulder out of place for such a long time gets uncomfortable. You are doing it and just getting colder and colder in freezing water like that without being able to move, and you lose your body heat fairly quickly. I must have blown twenty-five or thirty takes during the course of those two days. They would be shooting and all of a sudden I would inadvertently shiver or my teeth would chatter – and they would say, "CUT! The corpse is shivering here!"

Sometimes we would have to take a little break, and even though it was hotter than hell, they had to make a fire over on the bank. I would jump out of the water and go over and take my clothes off (keeping the cold wet clothes on didn't help), and I would wrap in a blanket and get warmed up by the fire while they set up the next shot. And then I would go back and get in the water. Pretty soon the crew were taking bets on how long I would make it before the next shiver.

The crew were really great guys. They treated me wonderfully and I couldn't have been in better hands. We dealt with all these adversities we had through humor. We had to. In the film crew union there's a special rate you get for water pay. If you are in four feet of water for X amount of time, there is added pay for that, and they would make jokes about it. Like what if you were in for 20 hours and there was only two feet of water. So we were always dealing with stuff like that. They really did take good care of me, but they did razz me a lot about blowing as many takes as I did.

When we had to move on to the actual eulogy, I had to be trussed up a bit and have rocks put on me. John Boorman wanted the shot to last long enough that they could sink me and have a graceful moment of silence for Drew's death. That became another problem as well. I had to breathe so surreptitiously that no one could ever see – and a couple of times they would say, "I saw his stomach move", or, "I saw him breathe" – so that took a lot of takes too. Then when they get to the point of actually sinking me in the water, and they wanted me to stay down long enough, luckily I have these rocks on me and I can hold onto these rocks to help keep me down. The problem was taking a deep enough breath that was not discernable so I could stay below the surface long enough for them to get the shot.

We had discussed this for a bit. John Boorman told me to stay down as long as I could and they would make it work. I don't know exactly how it happened, I don't know if I managed to get an extra big deep breath or if I went into some kind of zen mode or something... but when they sunk me down there I was holding on to a rock to keep me down and I stayed down SO long they sent guys down to get me. They thought they had lost me. John Boorman was actually kind of pissed off at me because he thought I was being a smart ass, but I wasn't. I was just staying down as long as I could...

Not an easy place to shoot a film...
a glimpse of the challenges that faced the crew every day.

TAKING A LESSON
FROM BURT REYNOLDS

I'd like to tell you a story about my first autograph. We had been shooting for, oh, I don't know, maybe a couple of weeks, and it was Sunday morning and we had the day off. I can remember that Burt and I were sharing a leisurely late breakfast, it must have been around ten or ten thirty in the morning. We were sitting in this restaurant, just the two of us. Now you have to realize that "Buddy" Reynolds was known in the South – he had played at the University of Georgia as a running back down there and he was still legendary in Georgia. He was also a big enough star by that time, having already done *Dan August*, *100 Rifles*, and been on *Gunsmoke*. But he was a superstar in Georgia.

So here we were in this restaurant having breakfast, and there were a couple of tables full of folks over across the room. You could see by the way they were all looking over that they had recognized Burt and were thrilled that he was there in the restaurant. Pretty soon this little boy who couldn't have been more than six or seven came sidling up to the table and very politely said, "Mr. Reynolds, could I get your autograph?"

I have to tell you this – every star in the world should take lessons from Burt Reynolds. I have never known any other major star or celebrity who was so kind and generous and friendly to his fans. Burt said, "Why yes, absolutely young man, come sit here in the booth with us", and he asked him his name and signed his autograph and visited with him. And I have to say this – I saw Burt do this hundreds of times, no matter what the circumstances, he always treated his fans wonderfully. If ever there was a guy whose personality was suited to being a star that people wanted to get autographs from, it was Burt Reynolds. Because he delighted in it too, or at least he made everybody think that he delighted in it, because he did it wholeheartedly.

So he signed the autograph for this young boy, and the boy was just getting down from out of the booth and Burt stopped him, sort of grabbed his shirt a little bit and said, "Listen – you might want to get THIS guy's autograph too." And the little boy said, "How come?" So Burt told him who I was, and said, "He's not famous yet, but we're doing a movie and he's going to be a big star someday, so you should maybe get his autograph." Well, the little boy wasn't too sure, but Burt had told him to do it, so he handed out this guest check for me to sign and I signed it. It was the very first autograph I had ever signed in my life and it was kind of a thrill. The little kid was forced into getting it, but nonetheless I signed it and we went back to our breakfast.

Pretty soon this little boy comes back and he's dragging his little sister, who is about four. The little boy says, "Mr. Reynolds, can she have your autograph?" and Burt again says of course, sat her down, asked her name, signed the autograph and put a little message on there for her, and thanked them for coming by. As they start to get down, the little boy says, "Wait, wait, WAIT!", and he pointed to me and said, "Get him too. He's nothing now, but he's going to be SOMEDAY!" So I signed two autographs in one day.

I know a lot of actors and movie stars and music stars that get mightily insulted when people come and ask them to sign a napkin or a guest check or just a little slip of paper. This is something that Burt taught me. They don't understand the essence of what signing a napkin or something like that is. Most of those people are not going to go and frame that napkin, they might even throw it away once they get outside. It might be the only thing they have to write on, but asking for an autograph gives them an excuse to come and have a conversation with a celebrity, a legitimate excuse where they feel they have a reason to be there, and a basis to start a conversation. They just want to be able to have some sort of social intercourse with this actor, this celebrity... and this napkin, this piece of paper gives them an excuse to have contact.

Any actor that doesn't understand that I think needs to go back and look at where that comes from. Burt Reynolds certainly understood and embraced it.

THEY SHOULD
RECOGNIZE ME!

Deliverance is one of the few novels that has been made into a film that I like both the novel and the film. For me, at least, if I like the book, then I normally hate the film. Or vice versa. The reason I liked both the book and the film of *Deliverance* is even though they are both telling exactly the same story, they are telling it in two completely different ways. The novel is written in first person. Everything is seen through Ed's eyes, Jon Voight's character. It's all told from his point of view. All his observations, all the things that are running through his mind and roiling up inside of him. . . . you can't really tell a film that way. So the film is told more from a third person point of view, an observation. Because of that, the nature of the two pieces are very different.

For instance, in the novel the big set piece, probably a hundred pages of the novel, is that climb up the mountain, almost like those movies where people's whole lives pass before their eyes. In the book, Ed's character tries to figure out where he fits in the scheme of things. He is going up there to possible death himself. It's really in a way the be-all and end-all of the philosophy of the book. Whereas in the film, the climb of the mountain is perhaps five minutes of film. We get that philosophy in a completely different way.

That's the critical difference between novels and plays versus film. Novels and plays are an active intellectual exchange between the author and the reader or the cast and the audience. Film is often times a visceral experience and visual experience - simultaneously. Those images just sort of get sucked in right into your insides and can bypass your brain for long periods of time. Eventually when you contemplate what was going on you get the intellectual exchange. You have the visceral reaction first, and then you get to have the intellectual reaction to it later. That's one of the key differences in film as opposed to novels and plays. You just experience them in a different realm.

Most people don't realize this, but Mary and my two sons are actually in *Deliverance*. If you recall at the end of the picture, after they made it down to Aintry, Ned's character says to Jon, "I don't think I'll see you for awhile". Jon is going to drive Drew's car back down to Atlanta just before the conversation with the sheriff, "Don't you guys come up here anymore"... he flips down the visor of Drew's car and there's a picture of Drew and his family. Mary at that time was finishing up her post-doc fellowship at Sloan Kettering and they didn't get to be in Georgia for long, but she took her vacation, and while she and the boys came down to visit me on the set, the production company came to me and asked if they could take a picture of my actual family and use it for the picture on the visor. It always gives me a bit of a start when I watch the film and they flip down the visor and there's Mary and my two sons.

As a side light to that – I'm not necessarily proud of this... but you have to realize this was my first film. It's hard to explain to kids what acting is. For a while my boys thought I worked at the airport because they took me there so often. I thought it was important for them to see my work, and since they were both in it. Brian was about ten and John was about five, so I felt that I could talk them through the bad stuff enough, and I broke down and Mary and I took them to see *Deliverance* when it opened in New York. We saw it at a matinee. It was one of the best reactions I've ever seen. We watched the film and the boys were cool with it. They got that I didn't really drown, they could reach over and pinch me, they knew that I was okay. They are bright kids, they understood the whole acting thing, so my fears were unfounded. All my angst over that was really for naught.

As we were leaving the film and we are walking into the lobby, John, who was five, had stopped and was standing and looking around with his hands on his hips. He seemed to be a MAD little kid. I asked him what was wrong, and he said, "Dad. I can understand why people don't recognize YOU because they dyed your hair black and they put you in glasses and they put a hat on you. I can understand that. But they should recognize ME!!" He was standing in the lobby waiting for people to come up and ask him for his autograph. And John is now 45 and doesn't get to forget that. We remind him of it.

The picture on the visor

I'VE GOT TO PAY
THE DOCTOR

I guess after we'd been shooting for maybe six weeks, there was a weekend when I had the day off and I went into town and actually I was talking with the editor. I'd gone by the editor's office, he wanted to show me some footage that we'd shot, and we needed to be able to go back and match the shot. John Boorman wanted me to go in and look at this footage so that I could see what I needed to do. I was in the editing office and talking with Tom Priestley, and was just leaving there and sort of really wasn't paying that much attention. We stood outside his office for maybe five or ten minutes just shooting the bull after I'd seen the footage, just basically visiting.

I looked up and coming down the road maybe fifty feet away from me was Billy Joe Redden, the kid that had played *Dueling Banjos* with me. I hadn't seen him for five or six weeks, and it was almost like a different world. He was walking along and he was limping terribly, as if he could hardly put any pressure on his right leg. He was sort of holding his knee and limping along, and I went running over to him and I said, "Billy, what's WRONG?" And he said, "Oh Ronny, I don't know, I was over there with old Tommy Ray and we was playing and we was going over this fence, and I fell down and I think I BROKE my leg, I gotta go see the doctor, it's just really BAD!" And I said, "Oh MAN, Billy, is there anything I can do for you? Can I take you somewhere?" And he said, "No, no, I'm almost there, it's just across the street over there, and I'm gonna go over and git it all taken care of, but listen Ronny, listen, you wouldn't happen to have five dollars 'til payday, would ya? Cause I need to go and pay the doctor!"

And I'm thinking, "Payday, I don't know WHAT he's talking about, there's no payday coming" – but I said, "Of course, of course", and I reached in my pocket, and I don't even know what I gave him, I think I may have even given him a twenty, and I said, "Just take care of yourself and let me know what's going on". He said, "Oh THANK you, Ronny, I'll pay you back soon's I get my next check", and so he went limping off and I was really concerned about him because it just really looked like he could hardly walk.

So he crossed the street there and I just turned back around to say goodbye to Tom, we were about to go. I look around and here was Billy Joe walking down the other side of the street, not a TRACE of a limp, just going down the road. He had obviously found his mark, I would have given him the money no matter what, but it goes to show what a great actor he really was because he had to have the money to get to the doctor. It was pretty funny, both Tom and I laughed about it, and of course Tom had to tell everybody else about it, and I got a fair amount of ribbing, although what do I care, about my naivete...

YOU DON'T NEED
MONEY FOR HAPPINESS

I guess it's time to talk about this a bit. We finished the film, obviously, and now I go back to Rye, New York, where Mary, the boys and I were living. My life just started changing drastically. I think the only way to really paint an accurate picture of that is to sort of tell you where I came from. Mary and I grew up in a small little town, Portales, New Mexico. Mary's family moved there when she was eleven, and I was fourteen. And we actually started going together when she was fifteen and I was eighteen, and eventually got married and had kids. You have to realize that we got married when Mary had just barely turned nineteen and had just finished her freshman year in college. I was on the eight year plan in college and was only a junior in college at that time. Then we had our first son. Brian was born eleven months later, right before Mary turned twenty.

So here we were, Mary was a chemistry major and I was majoring in theater, and we were in this little podunky school in Portales, New Mexico, at Eastern New Mexico University, and pretty much living hand-to-mouth with a small child and no real prospects. Mary and I were doing that typical thing that young married people do. As college students, we were putting off living our lives until sometime down the road... and then one night, during that year, we both realized sort of simultaneously that we were DOING exactly what we wanted to do. Mary wanted to get a PhD in Chemistry and I wanted to become a famous actor and folk singer, and we both realized that we were putting off living our lives because we didn't have any money or prospects. For us to achieve our goals we were going to have to live this life for a really good long time.

I can remember talking about it with Mary. We both sort of realized we were doing exactly what we wanted to do, we were extremely happy, we just didn't happen to have any money. And all of a sudden coming to that realization, we realized that we really didn't need money for our happiness. I know the difference between not having enough and being able to scrape by, and it was oddly freeing for both of us from that moment on. So we both sort of agreed and were affirmed in the fact that we were going to do exactly what we wanted and would achieve or pursue our dreams and goals. And if we had to make sacrifices or cut corners in terms of our own personal wealth, then that's what we would do.

We spent the next several years living that very life. Mary eventually graduated, I worked at a little summer theater in Colorado where we did melodramas until we got out of school. We both graduated in 1963 and Mary had a National Science Foundation Fellowship to Georgetown University. Maybe this it the time to talk about how brilliant Mary was. She never made a B in her life. The thing I admire more than anything else in the world in life is intelligence, and Mary was the most intelligent human being I've ever known. Anyway, she got this fellowship to Georgetown University and I tagged along to Washington, D.C., and managed to get hired by Arena Stage. As it turns out, Arena Stage, which is a really prestigious theater in Washington, D.C., is probably one of the MOST prestigious theaters in America outside of New York, with a wonderful repertory company and a tremendous reputation.

Once we got to Washington, D.C., I just sort of dropped by the theater one day, and as it turns out, Arena Stage was just that very year instituting a production intern program. Unbeknownst to me, they had advertised the year before, and they were going to accept six production interns. Now production intern is a glorified term for indentured servant. You were there to build the sets and do whatever else they wanted and occasionally you might get to play a role. Anyway, they had had hundreds of applications to fill these six spots as a production intern, and the criteria was that you had to have been a theater major and you had to be a college graduate. Well, I had just graduated when I dropped by, I didn't even know about this program. These six production intern spots had been awarded months ago, there was NO possibility of my getting one of those, I had just dropped by to see if I could be hired for any reason at all.

Well, that very day that I went by the theater, one of the interns that had been accepted had had to back out and cancel for some sort of emergency in their family, and they were not able to come and be a production intern. The season was about to start and the interns were supposed to arrive that week. As it turns out, there was an opening that very day, and I was there. So I got hired as this production intern for forty dollars a week. Between Mary's National Science Foundation Fellowship, which paid $2300 a year, and my $40 a week, we were now suffering real culture shock of rents because we are now living in the Washington, D.C. area.

You have to realize that when we were in school at Eastern New Mexico University, we were living in married student housing, what they called "Vetville". They had been built as old army barracks, and Mary and I were living in a one-bedroom furnished apartment in Vetville for $24 a month. So for us now coming to D.C., the rents were astronomical as far as we were concerned – we were still in abject poverty.

So I got this job and became a production intern. As it turns out, I was the only production intern that they asked back for the following year, and eventually I became an assistant stage manager there, and even then got to start playing some roles there. Although I have to tell you that it's hard, almost impossible, to make good where you started out. Especially in the mid-60's. If you were a theater actor, you were supposed to have a wonderful mid-Atlantic accent, certainly general American, and here I was from New Mexico, with a rather pronounced Southwestern drawl. Even though I worked diligently to get rid of that drawl, they never realized that. Other people can see your growth, but the people who saw you from the get-go couldn't. Even though I eventually became an assistant stage manager and went on to play some little roles, they actually encouraged me there to give up acting on two separate occasions.

Zelda Finchandler, who was the artistic director of Arena Stage, called me into her office and said, "Ronny – give it UP. We can get actors like you a dime a dozen in New York". And of course, she was right, at a moment's notice they could go to New York and get an actor. What's really hard to get, especially in regional theaters like that, are really good, dedicated technical people, and I was not necessarily that good when I went there. I thought the way to get them to give me a chance as an actor was to prove and show my value to them, and in a way, I sort of cut my own throat. I found out later there would be a role for a production intern in a show, and a director would say, "Well, I would like to use Ronny for this", and the technical people would say, "No, no, no, you can have anybody BUT Ronny", because I became too valuable backstage that they weren't about to let me on stage.

So I have to tell you at the end of six years at Arena Stage I could read a script and if there was going to be a role for me, whatever the smallest role that an Equity actor was going to play, that would be my role. As a matter of fact, the way I got those roles - I sort of blackmailed them. I told them I would stage manage three shows if I could act in three shows. My ego as an actor during that period was miniscule because I just had not had much success at all and the only encouragement I got was occasionally I would get to play a small role that I could shine in. I got to play Davidson in *Andersonville Trial* – he's only on stage for maybe ten or twelve minutes, but it's a wonderful role. I got cast in that - so occasionally even though I was getting no encouragement at all from the management and directors there, the other actors would come to me sometimes and say, "Man, you're GOOD!"

The way you learn to act is by doing the work. Even though they weren't casting me in the roles that I wanted to get, I would secretly cast myself in the role I thought I should have. I would go home and work on that character. I would come and watch rehearsals and watch the guy that was playing the role I wanted to play – sometimes I would take lessons from him or feel like I could do it better. In many ways I was working on those roles while I was building the sets and stage managing the shows...

YOU
DO NOW!

So... anyway, Mary eventually got her PhD in 1969, and by that time John had been born as well, so now we have two small boys. We were doing a production of *Indians* at Arena Stage, which they were then going to take to Broadway in the fall. I went to the people at Arena Stage because I was dedicated to being a stage actor. If they had offered me roles, I might STILL be at Arena Stage playing in plays.

I had a meeting with Zelda. She invited me back for the next year. The way they got the other actors to come back, they would offer them really meaty roles in three plays and more inconsequential roles in other plays. Well, I had never had any role that was really offered to me. So Zelda said, "Of course we'll have you back next year", and I said "Well, can you tell me ONE role that's going to be mine?" And she said, "NO, of course not, you'll just play what's left over", sort of cavalierly dismissing me. I was no longer stuck there because Mary was finished at Georgetown and I was being offered a tiny role in this play they were taking to Broadway. It wasn't any significant role at all, but I was being offered that to go to New York.

So I said to Zelda, "I don't care how big it is, you MUST offer me one role that's mine, I can know it's mine, and I can go home and work on it"... and she said, "ABSOLUTELY not. We're not going to do that." So I told her I couldn't come back. She really acted as if I had betrayed her in a sort of major way and actually didn't speak to me for the rest of the season, about two or three weeks. She felt like I had betrayed her and stabbed her in the back. I'm trying not to be bitter about that, but it's hard. Maybe her point of view of this is different than mine. But it seemed to me that I had given them an awful lot of stuff and just wasn't being rewarded in any way.

So anyway, Mary and I went to New York and I did this Broadway show, *Indians*, in which I played Jesse James. It was a pretty insignificant role, and Mary started her post-doc at Sloan Kettering. The thing that was significant about all this was that there was a guy playing the senator in the play, Tom Aldrich, a wonderful man. He actually helped Mary and me find our house out in Rye, New York, because he was living in Mamaroneck, only a few miles down the road. Tom and I rode into the city every day during the run of *Indians* and while we were coming in to the city, Tom got offered a directing job for Joseph Papp. Joseph Papp was a legendary icon of the theater in New York, he did *Shakespeare in the Park, Hair*, etc. – he was Mr. Theater in New York. Not Broadway theater, but Mr. Artistic Theater. Tom got this opportunity to direct this brand new play and there was a role in it that he thought I might be good in, but there was no money in it. I was FLOORED, it was a leading role in a play, and of course I wanted to do it.

I did this play with Marty Sheen, Charles Durning, Harris Yulin, and we just ran for ten performances at the Public Theater downtown, totally free. From those ten performances, I must have gotten two hundred phone calls from agents, producers and directors all of a sudden noticing ME as an actor. As a matter of fact, that's how I got my first agent.

One night we were playing and this little tiny woman came backstage, she couldn't have been more than four foot eight, really tiny. She was Miss Audrey Woods, Tennessee Williams' agent. She wasn't even an actor's agent, she was a literary agent. She came back and said, "Young man, WHO's your agent?" And I said, "I don't have an agent", and she said, "You do NOW!". She was the head literary agent at ICM, and went back to ICM and told all of the agents there that they had to go and see the play. She forced them all and she wanted me signed to the agency. From six years of not even getting walk-on's at Arena Stage, now ALL this – I still hadn't really done anything in New York other than this one workshop show and an inconsequential show on Broadway, and all of a sudden there's a buzz around town. I'm sort of the new young Turk around New York City. When Lynn Stalmaster came to town looking for good unknown actors, I was recommended to him by the people at Joe Papp's theater. So in many ways, that was the break of a lifetime for me.

Joe just believed in me so much, even sometimes when I wasn't working, he would sneak a hundred bucks under the table to me just to keep me alive – so I'm forever grateful to Joe. That's the sort of background of me when I got *Deliverance*.

Now *Deliverance* is coming out and I'm being offered things that I didn't even know about, that I didn't even know existed. And I'm also now not even going through the casting or reading process. For years I didn't know any casting directors because as a result of *Deliverance*, I was just offered roles. My agents would just call up and the producer or director would have seen *Deliverance* and would say "We WANT Ronny for this".

Where it all Started...
Dueling Banjos

THE
GUERILLA SHOT

Even though *Deliverance* is the quintessential action/adventure movie, and it became such a huge hit and such an iconic film, I think one of the things people sometimes miss is that it is an artistic endeavor that most of those genres of films don't get to. There are so many places we've talked a little bit about things that happened almost serendipitously, but the thing about that film is there are other things that happened purely through the genius of John Boorman and Vilmos Zsigmond, who was the brilliant cinematographer that shot the film. One of the things they decided right from the very beginning was to desaturate the film, so that there were no vivid colors. The film is in color, but it has a muted color almost like black and white. They also very consciously shot the film strictly in earth tones. We never shot if the sun was out, we always shot only under cloud cover, so you never see blue sky in the film. If we were shooting and the sun came out, they would cut the camera.

And also here's a way that it paid off. Only on a subliminal level did people get it. You never see the color red in the entire film until the rapist is shot with that arrow, and then there's just this trickle of blood going down the shaft of that arrow. And even though that red is muted, it jumps at your eyes in a way that you just couldn't have imagined before. Those kinds of things really paid off. The climbing scene at the mountain when Jon Voight is climbing up – they purposely desaturated that SO much that it almost looked like surrealistic shadows playing everywhere. The juxtaposition of having this ultra naturalism that we've been able to achieve in the film, coupled with this surrealism, made for a really artistic take on everything.

I can't emphasize enough the importance of John Boorman's vision and having Vilmos shoot the film. In 1971, I think because of changing union rules, there was a big fight going on in those days of who could operate the camera. One of the last things that the director of photography ever wanted to give up was being the person who actually looked through the lens of the camera, the one who framed the shot. For some reason, through union negotiations or whatever, that was being given over to the first assistant camera operator. This was in the days before video assist. With video assist now, they have a video camera hooked up and you can actually see the same thing the camera lens is seeing, and the director can stand off to the side and see how the shot is being framed all through the take. But in those days, we didn't have video assist, so because of that the director had to stand as close as he could to the camera lens during the actual take, and he had to rely on the director of photography to know if he got it.

By this time, the camera operator was doing it, which was another layer, and the one operating the camera was the one who was actually getting to frame the movie. And that's a huge thing that none of our guys wanted to give up. Consequently, and I hope I'm not telling stories out of school here, but Vilmos sort of refused to give that up. He operated nearly every shot in the entire film and so we always knew the shot was framed and the lighting was in exactly the way that he wanted it to be.

Later there have been several other directors of photography who have gotten in some trouble because they didn't want to give up actually looking into the lens. For my money, that's probably the reason for the whole concept of how the video assist came into being, so everybody could certainly see exactly how the shot was being composed. You wouldn't have to rely on one person, especially if that person was two or three levels removed from the director and the director of photography.

There's another thing – and I hardly know how to talk about this – but I think it did lend itself to an artistic integrity about the film. I've had a lot of discussions with people who thought that this particular shot was in some way an exploitation. I'm certainly aware of the claim that someone might have thought that it's exploitive, but in the end I think the artistic merits overweigh that view. If you recall, when Jon Voight and Burt Reynolds are driving to the Griner brothers to get them to drive the cars down to Aintry, they go up to this one building, and just before they are about to knock, Burt's character hears a noise and he walks down to the Griner brother who is working on a car and that's where the shot is going. Jon's character glances into a window that's there, and inside the window is an ancient old grandmother sitting there knitting, and sitting with a horribly deformed little girl who couldn't be over three or four. She is a pitiful looking little girl who has just tiny stumps of arms and legs, and is sitting there beautifully innocent and heartbreaking.

That was a shot that they actually sort of stole in a way. When we were shooting the *Dueling Banjos* scene at that service station, and we were up on the porch setting up that shot, the camera man looked in and John Boorman saw this woman and this little girl there, and they sort of stole that shot through the window. It certainly didn't work for that particular scene, so they set it up at the Griner brothers so they could use it. Obviously when I said they "stole that shot", I meant they shot through the window and didn't go in and disturb anybody. It is sort of what is called a guerilla shot, with no lighting or staging. Certainly they got permission to use it, and the old woman and the little girl were paid handsomely, so in terms of that, they weren't exploited. A lot of people who saw that thought we shouldn't show that, but I think it takes the film even more into a realm of naturalistic place. It sets up the experience otherworldly that there is this mountain man existence in a way that you couldn't do in other films of this genre. It's what Jim Dickey calls the "land of people with nine fingers". Other action/adventure films never had those kind of touches, never had that kind of underlying pathos, and it put the film on a different level than films like this have been.

Also, since we are talking about this being of a different genre of film, one of the things that made this film such a widely-acclaimed film and touched so many chords was that for the very first time men were put in a position that women have had to deal with for years – this whole idea of rape. In a very naturalistic, animalistic way, men had to deal with the concept of rape, and that made a lot of people squirm and made this film hard to watch on a lot of levels. It is like watching a terrible accident – you want to look away, but you couldn't do it. It's like watching a train wreck. You had to watch it as much as you could.

Because of that approach that we had, it ties in directly with John Boorman's idea about the score and the soundtrack in the film. The only music in the whole film is variations on the *Dueling Banjos* theme. It's played in a minor key, variations here and there, but always a reiteration of that basic theme. The only other music at all in the film is at the campfire that first night we are out. My character Drew sits and plays his guitar and sings an old folksong called *Moonshiner's Lament*, a folksong that I knew. When we got down to Georgia, John Boorman asked me if I had a song to sing for that. I remembered that song, so I sang it. Over the years I've had hundreds of people write and want to know the lyrics to that song and I'm afraid I sang about all of it I knew. I only knew sort of one and a half verses of *Moonshiner's Lament*. Anyway, that little piece is the only other music that's in the show.

That's the same minimalist naturalistic approach. Normally in a film like this you would have big exciting scores, especially when they are going down through the rapids – and I don't mean to put down those scores, because music is incredible for creating tension – but this was an intentional artistic touch that put it in a different category than other films...

THE
LOVE NOTE

Now I have to talk about my first encounter with the "sexual perks" of being a movie celebrity. Mary and I... well, anyone that knows me knows that I married the love of my life, and I was the most married man you've ever known. It would never occur to me to look at any other woman. I'm not being disingenuous either. I've been around and I'm not THAT spectacular-looking, and women had never ever come on to me anyway. So all of a sudden, I'm down in Georgia – and part of it is that there are so many women that are trying to get to Burt Reynolds and it seems that they are coming out of the woodwork. I didn't all of a sudden become sexier overnight, and I really to this day sort of don't quite fathom what happens. There is something about being a movie star that certain people find sexually attractive. Even when Mary came down to visit the set, women would come up and practically throw themselves at me. It became a thing that you eventually learn to deal with. In my other films through the years, there's been a certain group of people that find movie actors sexy, and therefore you learn to deal with that.

I had certainly never encountered that when we were doing *Deliverance*. I am basically a fairly shy person about those kinds of things. I've never dated another girl other than Mary, and haven't been in that dance of courtship except with her. It really put me ill at ease. On one hand it was flattering and good for my ego – but on the other hand it was just bewildering and I didn't really quite know how to deal with it. Now having said all that – this is all leading up to this trick we played.

Once we got down to Georgia and by the time we had been there for a few weeks, the four of us had become fast friends and were spending so much time together that we really had a sort of easy comraderie going. What we discovered was that Burt Reynolds was the practical joker of the world. If he could find some way to pull a trick on you or do some joke, then he would, and he was forever pulling jokes, especially on Ned and me because we were the novices. We didn't know anything. He's actually the one who told us we were shooting in sequence and how lucky we were. So he was always occasionally pulling our legs, but the rest of the time giving us useful information. We kept wanting to find some way to get back at him.

Ned had come down to Georgia, but his wife Belinha was still at Arena Stage in Washington, D.C. finishing up the season there. So she didn't come to Georgia until we were three or four weeks down there. We picked her up and Ned and I hatched up this joke to pull on Burt. The thing you need to know about Burt – not only did women seek him out, he sought the women out as well. If there were any pretty girls on the set, Burt would be there in about twenty seconds. It was fun to watch him go, because he was the master at this. Who knew where it would lead? Belinha had come in the night before so Ned and I hatched up this whole big plot. We composed this letter. Belinha was coming out to the set the next day for lunch, and she showed up about ten o'clock in the morning. She is beautiful and happened to be six or seven months pregnant, but gorgeous... and of course, pretty soon, here came Burt.

We worked it out with her. First of all, she paid no attention to Burt, NONE. She acted as if he didn't exist, and he kept being there near her, and she started asking "Do you know Ronny?" And he looked totally puzzled and said "You mean Ronny Cox??" She said, "Yes, I saw him in a play in Washington, D.C., and he doesn't even know me but I have just been in love with him forever – do you know him?" And Burt said "Yeah, I know him... ." and she said "Oh, oh, OH, I have this note, I heard he was here, I have this note, would you give him this note for me PLEASE?" So he said okay and took the note. Ned and I had composed this note and it said: "Dear Mr. Cox, I have loved you forever and I want to be with you, and I only came to the set to see you, I don't even know the other actors at all, I just want to spend some time with you." She gave the note to Burt in the morning, and when we broke for lunch, we are now sitting at the table and Ned has ostensibly introduced her to me, and she is sitting with me and we are having a discussion. Burt is sitting on the other side of the table just beside himself, he can't believe this beautiful girl is essentially hitting on me and carrying on. We keep talking and every now and then Burt would say something, and she kept ignoring him. She didn't have anything to do with him.

Finally as lunch is over and he is walking away, he holds out the note and says "Ronny, this is for you.", and hands me the note. He had held on to it all morning, and had obviously read it and was disgruntled. We didn't have the nerve not to let him in on the joke.

I am reticent to tell this story a little bit but... Burt was always playing practical jokes, and one night he came running over to my house and he said "Ronny, get your guitar, come with me!" I said "Why?" and he said "There's three Girl Scout troops over here that are camping out, and their counselors have invited us! They are HOT, and I need someone with a guitar who can play music!" I said "Burt, give me a break!" – we had to go to work the next day, and I wanted him to go get Ned or Jon, and he said no, they couldn't play the guitar. And I said "Burt, I'm MARRIED!" and he said "I don't care, these girls are for ME, I just want you there playing background music!" Needless to say, I didn't go. Burt was mightily pissed off at me for not going with him to serenade him with the Girl Scouts. When I said "Girl Scouts, we'll get ARRESTED!", he said "I'm after the COUNSELORS, you idiot, not the Girl Scouts!"...

THE
GOLDFISH BOWL

For all the really wonderful marvelous things that happened, especially for me and for Ned, and for the film-going public in general – I think we made a truly remarkable film, if you will, and not only a popular action/adventure film, but an art film as well. However, there are some drawbacks that I think I have to address a little bit. For one thing, for all intents and purposes we almost spoiled that pristine river. Because, as I said before, we had to use four wheel drive or sometimes even caterpillars to get us down to the river or to get us out, and it was such a virgin piece of the wilderness. Once the film came out and people realized that we had been canoeing this river in Georgia, it struck such a romantic chord (no pun intended) for a lot of guys – they wanted to go and challenge themselves on that river. So now they started finding all kinds of ways to get down to that river.

Also, since my character drowned in the river, they had to start putting up all kinds of signs along the way about the class of the rapids and caution. They essentially had to take away the wilderness quality of that river in the effort to keep people from drowning. So many people would just get in the river without knowing what was around the next bend. You can really get in trouble that way. I don't even know quite how to talk about this, but after that film came out that year, I guess because Drew died in the picture, for some reason people felt it was important to send me all this material. I must have gotten hundreds of letters detailing all the people who drowned. They just felt they were kindred spirits, a lot of these letters were telling the same story from newspaper clippings and such. I just got a plethora of mail from fans and people like that who wanted to let me know that other people had died doing that as well.

Also banjo sales went through the roof. You couldn't buy a banjo that year, a lot of people credit the *Dueling Banjos* scene with a resurgence in bluegrass music in many ways. And canoe sales went up through the roof too. I think you could argue that the popularity of whitewater canoeing almost came as a direct result of that film. The liability is all the people who drowned from trying to do it.

There is another liability I think about. For a whole lot of people, it solidified in their mind the whole "cracker" nature of anyone from the South, the whole hillbilly inbred stereotype that people came to think about the South. Anyone from Georgia or down in the South there were sort of tainted with that brush of just being illiterate. It went a long way to fostering that stereotype. The opposite side of that coin is that a whole lot of people down there, the Southerners, didn't recognize that we were telling a very particular story about a particular area, and they felt that we were casting terrible aspersions on them and they resented that too. There was a source of tension that came from this movie.

Deliverance exacerbated that whole sort of dichotomy that we've all come to realize now. Of course that was right after the civil rights act passed. The South was turning from Dixie "crats" into Republicans and any sort of outsider was a suspect to begin with. That made it easier for the liberal North to say well, they're all just redneck idiots down there, and neither one is true, obviously – some of the most wonderful people in the world are down there, some of my closest friends.

In the summer of 1971 I got my first real taste of Southern politics. It's no secret that I'm a really left-wing liberal Democrat – I've been accused of being somewhere to the left of Mao Tse Tung. I try not to impose that on anybody else. Here we were in north Georgia, a rather conservative state, especially in that time. The unit publicist from Warner Brothers, a wonderful guy named Vernon White was there doing all the publicity stuff for the movie. Vernon was a cool hip guy who I've know through the years and eventually he became Kris Kristofferson's manager.

I had a little rented Volkswagen bug I was using to go back and forth from the Kingwood Country Club where we were staying. It was seven or eight miles out of town, and each of us had a car rather than a production driver, we needed some way to get into town. The other guys had rather more fancy cars than I did, but I was happy with my little bug. It was bright yellow and pretty soon everybody got to know my little yellow VW bug driving around.

Now remember, this was 1971, so we were gearing up for the election in 1972. Vernon White showed up and in the night he somehow put a bumper sticker on my VW bug. It read "LICK DICK in 72". I didn't even KNOW it was on there! As I said before, I had a rather good relationship with all the people in town, so I would be driving my yellow bug and everyone would wave to me or acknowledge me in some way or another. All of a sudden, people are honking at me and shaking their fists at me, and guys are driving by and giving me the finger – and I can't figure out why I am suddenly persona non grata. So I get out of the car and look down and see this bumper sticker, "LICK DICK in 72", and needless to say, I needed to get that off!

It was an eye-opener, such a boon to me, knowing what it was like to be a celebrity for the first time. I had lived my whole life in total anonymity, justifiably so up until then, as an unknown. I hadn't achieved anything yet, and just because I was in a movie all of a sudden, people were noticing what I was doing, paying attention to what I was doing. It was the first time in my life that I began to realize what a fishbowl especially big stars live under. I've had a certain amount of celebrity as an actor, but certainly not in that aspect. To go from no one caring or paying attention to what you were doing, and now suddenly wherever you went in town, in a grocery store, getting a haircut, going to a movie, people were noticing you and treating you in a way that was sometimes good, sometimes bad – but always in a way you felt like you could no longer just be you. It was really disconcerting at first not knowing how to deal with that. That's why I appreciate Burt Reynolds so much – he knew how to handle that part of celebrity better than anyone on earth, and actually did it with grace and a certain amount of relishing on his part.

For Ned and I, it was all of a sudden. You felt like you couldn't go anywhere and go have any bit of privacy. I met some people down there, wonderful people, Tom and Marilyn McNeely. They had a house out on Lake Rabun away from the hubbub, and they would invite me out to their house just to get away from any sort of scrutiny. It was such a haven to be able to just be Ronny if only for maybe a day, to be able to lie on the lake and not feel like you were in a goldfish bowl.

Shooting the film was really hard arduous work, and we worked long hours and we were on the water and it was debilitating. But we were all young guys and happy to do it. So doing that all week, and then having to face your down time as being a sort of trophy on display everywhere you went wore on you almost as much. Being able to go out to Tom and Marilyn's place on the lake was so great. They loved music and I took my guitar out there and we would play. Marilyn's younger sister was an airline stewardess named Ann Delong. She was sort of my first groupie I think that I ever had. If she had a weekend off, she would come out to visit her sister and brother-in-law, and I'm not suggesting anything happened – I was a very happily married man – but it was good for my ego.

Here again, I don't know really how to come to grips with that, I know that initially I thought that she was being a groupie for all the wrong reasons, just because I happened to be a "movie star". Over the course of two or three weekends, I was able to see that she just enjoyed my music, more than any sort of actor celebrity – and anyone who loves my music has gone a long way to endearing themselves to me. Having Tom and Marilyn and Marilyn's sister really appreciate my music meant a lot to me. Somehow it means way more to me for people to enjoy my music and to think I'm a good musical entertainer than being an actor. I think it's because when you are an actor, you are playing a character and are part of the ensemble. There are certain things you have to do. I love doing it, don't get me wrong – but my music is me.

I'm the straw that gets to stir the drink. If I choose to do a song, I choose to do it my way.

AND IN THE END...

I want to talk a little about the writing process of this book. I'm a storyteller. The way I've always written, whether it's screenplays or songs or whatever – I just sort of sit and ruminate and sort of find my way through like that.

My wife Mary used to say that the way I write is that I sit around and talk and make up stuff and hem and haw and then eventually someone has to translate that into English. That's sort of how I planned to do this book, and since Mary's not here, obviously I needed to have someone to translate it into English. That person is Barbara Bowers. I can't tell you enough about how wonderful I think she is. As a writer, she's smart, she knows how to write, she knows how to tell a story. And if anyone can make sense out of what I'm talking about, then she can do that.

So hopefully, everybody will enjoy these stories I've told. And if there is any literary merit to any of this, then that's Barbara's fault.

I've had a forty year career that is almost completely dependent upon that one remarkable lucky break of getting *Deliverance*. I think that's one of the reasons – I know it's the reason – that *Deliverance* means so much to me, and why these stories of *Deliverance* still resonate in me as though it were yesterday. It's forty years later, and I'm still sitting here marveling at all these remarkable things that have happened to me and for me. I've had a fantastic career, not that I've ever been a big star... in all honesty, I don't care about being a big star. What I really care about is being offered the good roles to play, and I've certainly gotten to do that. There's no way I can adequately articulate how much this remarkable film has meant...but with these stories, I have tried.

October 2011

Budding Author

I love this photo

CPSIA information can be obtained at www.ICGtesting.com
Printed in the USA
BVOW031419271112

306168BV00008BA/580/P